In the Faraway Mountains and Rivers

In the Faraway Mountains and Rivers

Harukanaru Sanga ni

Writings of the University of Tokyo Students
Killed in World War II

Compiled by Tōdai Gakusei Jichi-kai Senbotsu Gakusei Shuki Hensan
Iinkai (Committee for Compiling the Writings of the University of Tokyo
Students Killed in the War, the University of Tokyo Student Council)

Translated by

Joseph L. Quinn, S. J.
Midori Yamanouchi

Scranton: The University of Scranton Press

Harukanaru Sanga ni was first published by the University of Tokyo Co-op, Publishing Department in 1947, and later by the University of Tokyo Press in 1951. This translation is from the newly designed edition published in 1989.

Library of Congress Cataloging-in-Publication Data

Harukanaru sanga ni. English.
   In the faraway mountains and rivers = Harukanaru sanga ni : writings of the University of Tokyo students / compiled by Todai Gakusei Jichi-kai Senbotsu Gakusei Shuki Hensan Iinkai (Committee for Compiling the Writings of the University of Tokyo Students Killed in the War, University of Tokyo Student Council) ; translated by Joseph L. Quinn, Midori Yamanouchi.
      p. cm.
   Translation is from newly designed ed., 1989.
   ISBN 1-58966-108-7 (pbk.)
   1. World War, 1939-1945--Personal narratives, Japanese. 2. College students--Japan--Correspondence. 3. Students and war--Japan. 4. Tokyo Daigaku--Students. I. Quinn, Joseph L. II. Yamanouchi, Midori, 1928- III. Todai Gakusei Jichikai. Senbotsu Gakusei Shuki Hensan Iinkai. IV. Title.
   D811A2 .H313 2005
   940.54'8252--dc22

                                                                    2005042224

Distribution:

University of Scranton Press
Chicago Distribution Center
11030 S. Langley
Chicago, IL 60628

PRINTED IN THE UNITED STATES OF AMERICA

CONTENTS

PREFACE

Representing as I do only a minority share in the labors which have resulted in this volume, the person to whom premier acknowledgment must be made is quite clear—my colleague and coauthor, Dr. Midori Yamanouchi. In many ways uniquely qualified for first proposing and then directing the entire enterprise, both Midori's access to our primary sources and her frequently very difficult decoding of this material formed the indispensable bedrock underpinning the whole project.

Of course her gratitude as well as my own goes out to those now legendary young men who were moved to share the agonies of their ordeal throughout the Second World War, and who in doing so all but established a new literary genre.

> The written history of the world is largely a history of war-fare, because the states within which we live came into existence largely through conquest, civil strife, or struggles for independence.
>
> – John Keegan, *A History of Warfare*

The material we are dealing with makes up part of that "written history of the world" referred to in the Keegan epigraph. Elsewhere, the same author suggests that there is no such thing as "the nature of war," and perhaps he is correct. What is certain is that, of all the theories and treatises devoted to the subject—including the most famous, Carl von Clausenitz's *On War*—no book ever written has come close to being fully satisfactory.

Our authors are not, and never claimed to be, great writers, but they have nevertheless proven most satisfactory in illuminating certain aspects of the war about which Westerners have been consistently mis-informed. The suicide pilots whom we came to know as "kamikazes" provide an excellent example. From the first, this late attempt to turn the war around was recognized as the deadly menace it was, and our newspapers abused the Kamikazes as fanatics, madmen, drug addicts, and other bad things, but several of the pages you are about to read throw something of a different light onto the matter. Although we probably cannot avoid finally judging them as ignorant or misled, or both, neither can we avoid recognizing a certain magnificence about such willingness to throw away their still very young lives. —However grudgingly, the recognition might just breed some admiration not only for the young men themselves, but also for the culture that produced them.

Herman Wouk remains one of the most astute and talented fictive commentators on the Second World War, and near the conclusion to his *War and Remembrance* he himself harks back to a better book by a much bigger man.

> In Leo Tolstoy's *War and Peace*, which all military men have read (or should have), there are some pretty questionable historical and military theories; among them, the notion that strategic and tactical plans do not actually matter a damn in war. The variables are infinite, confusion reigns, and chance governs all. So says Tolstoy. Most of us have had that feeling in battle, one time or another. Still, it is not so. The battles of Grant and Spruance—to take American instances—show solid results from solid planning. However, Tolstoy makes one telling point: that victory turns on the individual brave spirit in the field, the man who snatches the flag, shouts "Hurrah!" and rushes forward when the issue is in doubt, that is a truth we all know too.

In the Pacific War, and even in the face of defeat, each of our authors was that man.

J. L. Q.

——————————————

ACKNOWLEDGMENTS

When the horrendous Pacific War was over, the first thought for those of us who survived, as we gazed at almost totally destroyed cities, was "Somehow I did not get killed. And now . . . ?" Our hearts were heavy about those who were killed in the war, both in the battlefield and at home. This book, *Harukanaru Sanga ni* (*In the Faraway Mountains and Rivers*), a collection of writings of the fallen University of Tokyo students, was published in 1947 when it was still a very difficult time: everything was extremely short of supply, not only food, but even the paper for publishing books. I vividly recall how deeply I was touched by the book, and it deepened my sorrow over how those fine, able men from the University of Tokyo had to die in the war that they could not control and did not want. I remember that, in the months prior to the end of the war, following right after the daily news, we heard several farewell speeches of those young men as they prepared to leave for their final sorties. Even after the war ended in defeat, my family continued to be utterly concerned over the fate of my older brother, whom the army, though defeated, kept from returning home for several weeks. We were so blessed with the good fortune to get him back, but many of my friends were not.

Since I came to the United States for my graduate study in the 1950s, I heard many Americans, even well-intentioned ones, speak of Japanese soldiers, and "kamikaze" pilots in particular, as if they were mindless and robot-like, who simply followed a command, dove to a target and died. It hurt me because that is a terrible misconception, and so I wanted Americans to read this book. But I realized this book, although so well-known, had not been translated into English. And, finally, a few years ago, I thought I should take up the task: I wanted so much to give each of those young men a human face. When I seriously thought about doing so, I realized that *Harukanaru Sanga ni* was no longer available. So I decided to translate *Kike Wadatsumi no Koe* (*Listen to the Voices from the Sea*), a more inclusive work, in the sense that it contained students from other universities, that replaced *Harukanaru Sanga ni* a couple years later. With a wonderful collaborator, Rev. Joseph L. Quinn, S.J., the task was completed and *Listen to the Voices from the Sea* was published in 2000. For the translation of this title, *Harukanaru Sanga ni*, I owe immensely to Professor Okada of the Wadatsumi Society, who so graciously made a copy available, so I was able to do what I wanted to do in the first place. My special attachment to this work is due to the fact that my older brother was also a student of the University of Tokyo, Faculty of Jurisprudence, and, if he were only a half year older, he may have very well shared the same fate as the authors of this book. Those young men at our Japanese universities were mobilized in 1943 to fight the war which we all knew was already lost. I wanted so much to give each of those young men a human face: and if by so doing I could perhaps change American perception of them, I would be honored. After the publication of *Listen to the Voices from the Sea*, I received many letters from readers from both sides of Pacific Ocean. I am deeply touched by those letters, and I truly appreciate that the readers shared their reactions with me. I hope this new title will give the reader even more insight into about what those intelligent young men, the students of the University of Tokyo, were like: such as what they were reading and what they were thinking. They had stood opposed to the aggressive Japanese military and the expansionists, yet they had to fight the final stage of a losing war, hoping to preserve their beloved fatherland and to protect their families whom they loved. I sincerely hope that the reader will feel their sense of humanity.

Just as for the earlier work, *Listen to the Voices from the Sea*, a translation of *Kike Wadatsumi no Koe*, I am most grateful to my collaborator, Fr. Joseph L. Quinn, S.J., professor of English literature at the University of Scranton, who made the final version so great. I asked him because I wanted to avoid the common problem of awkwardness so often found in many translations, and I knew him to be the best. I am grateful beyond words that he worked with me again on this title. I am most appreciative of the University of Tokyo Press for its gracious permission for me to translate this title. And, most certainly, I owe immensely to Professor Hiroyuki Okada of the Wadatsumi Society not only for official matters such as granting me the translation rights but also for his wonderful encouragement and gracious friendship. And I am truly indebted to Mrs. Fumie Ogawa, my close friend since our college days, for if it were not for her connecting me with the Society. There were also many others to whom I owe sincere gratitude, such as Dr. Harold Baillie, Mr. Arthur Watres, Mrs. Gloria Sottile, and Mr. Michael Suetta, for their invaluable assistance. Last, but not the least, most certainly I am grateful as ever to Fr. Richard W. Rousseau, S.J., and his successor, Mr. Jeffrey L. Gainey, the publisher, University of Scranton Press, and Ms. Patricia A. Mecadon, production manager.

M. Y.

DEDICATION TO THE STUDENTS
KILLED IN THE WAR

Shigeru Nanbara[1]

We are here with grief in our hearts to honor you, our young friends, students, and staff, who would never return from the field of battle forever only because you left us to fight in the war.

As we look back over the last few years, how did we citizens find ourselves in this predicament? We seemed to be wandering in a dream world full of chaos, confusion, and madness. But it was real: we were swept up in a torrent of historical fact—in which some serious things kept happening one after another, and as a consequence, we were beset by worries and anxieties, tension and excitement, despair and sorrow, all interwoven. The single-minded pursuit of the war was planned by a small number of ignorant, reckless, ambitious, ultranationalists and militarists; and it became clearly evident that the entire nation was headed for disaster.

In spite of the victorious news at the outbreak of the Pacific War, (which followed the long China Conflict,[2] and which in the end determined the fate of the Japanese people), the mood of the University was somber and you, the students, were consciously not inflamed by it. As the saying goes, "Even though they whistled so loud, you did not dance to it." Indeed, for those who seriously searched for the truth in an environment of scholarly pursuits, their rationality and conscience did not allow them to do so. Especially, those immersed in the study of philosophy, political science, law, and economics knew too well that the rush of events was reckless and utterly irrational. You, university students, in silence simply followed your long-cherished desire, to discharge the duty as the students; and we the instructors continued to lecture and teach that.

However, once the mobilization order was given, the special privileges of the students were abolished. Replacing your pens with swords, with dignity and courage, you marched off to war. Unlike the

---

[1] President of the University of Tokyo in 1947.

[2] The undeclared war between China and Japan, which began with the Marco Polo Bridge Incident in 1937 and lasted until the Pacific War, was called China *Jihen* (incident, conflict) as it was never declared a war. It followed the Manchurian Conflict, which started in 1931.

response observed in other countries, in our very large student body, not even a single student refused to follow the order and avoided the citizens' duty to serve the nation. All of you loyally followed the nation's mandate and order. I do not know if we, who always taught you that course of action, were right or wrong. And, you did not simply follow the orders blindly, as a horse led by a bit, either. How courageously and in high spirits, with burning passion of patriotism to serve the nation, you left us once the students were mobilized to fight the war on that unforgettable day in November last year. How bravely and gallantly you fought, risking your lives. Across the broad expanses of the war you performed your duty as soldiers in endless battlefields and military posts. The pains and difficulties you endured during that time can never be known except by those who shared that experience with you.

I know for certain that you were quite different from the ordinary soldiers of limited vision and experience. You were warriors and students at the same time. You did not fight with a dogmatic and fanatic "unfailing belief in victory." I know that you hoped for the victory of justice and truth above all, even though you were determined that "we must win," once the war was decided upon. Unfortunately, however, justice and truth were not for us to enjoy; they were for America and Great Britain. This is not to say that "The victor is just;" rather, it was the inexorable unfolding of history, "the judgement of rationality." We, together, have no choice but to accept that verdict in the midst of the pain of the defeat of war.

You did not see with your own eyes the most cursed day in the long history of our country—August 15th of last year. The painful anger we felt, that indignation, was not aimed at the enemy but, rather, at ourselves. The misery that we have been suffering ever since and the even greater inner wounds are truly "the cross of reality" that our people must bear. We have no choice but to endure and persevere. We are now passing through a great ordeal that exceeds that of the war itself.

However, gentlemen, what I should like to tell you is that a glorious new dawn is ready to shine upon us. Now, our nation is going through the greatest political, social, and spiritual transition in our history. By means of that, we must build a new Japan truly dedicated to peace and morality and create a new Japanese culture. Indeed this is the greatest undertaking which we, the university and its students, must seek to achieve with the whole force of our being: we must endeavor to focus our goals and culture on "rationality" so as to deal more effectively with the grim realities we now face.

Our university carries a heavy responsibility in reconstituting our country with a focus on humane and civilized endeavor. While you were away fighting in the war, those of us who remained continued our labors and studies under extremely difficult conditions; and at the same time, we were seeking the truth in an endeavor to maintain civilized values and prepare ourselves for today. During that time, we were under many fire bombings, and so many of our people gave their lives trying to save the university from the fires. We shall never forget these precious lives lost in unrecognized sacrifice. After so many of the students left for the war, the university became quiet and lonely: there were times when no one was seen under the rows of gingko trees.

After the end of the war, somehow, from distant parts, our friends gathered: with what joy we welcomed them! There were those who left for the war at the same time you did, but returned home, enduring shame worse than death; but they are here to join the new fight, the great endeavor of reviving the university and rebuilding the fatherland. It is our deepest and eternal sorrow, though, that while almost all of them have come back now, there are so many brilliant ones whom we will never see again in any of the classrooms or research offices.

I often think of those of you who kindly came to see us to say good-bye as you were leaving for the war front, and, that turned out to be the last farewells. Countless times we shed tears over what you wrote to us so touchingly of your deep inner feelings from the battlefield. Immersed in the military regimen on battlefields so far from home, you expressed your longing and appreciation for the university, the search for truth, and even for us, your professors. We often feel the impulse to call out your names, one by one, and seek the solace of higher powers.

Moreover, we cannot help grieving in pain and sympathy as human beings and as compatriots when we think of the yearning of your parents, who brought you into this world and brought you up, and of your sisters and brothers, who all shared joys together at the family hearth, particularly when this war was a silent teacher [reminding us of the value of human relationships].

These, however, were simply the sacrifices that our nation required of us, citizens, for prosecuting the war—nothing but the sacrifices required for the collective sins and our national follies. You, rather than your compatriots, did not hesitate to play that role, and went to the place of death with a smile. It is as if you were saying to us, "Whom should I hate and whom should I blame at this point? Students and compatriots all, with a single heart, please tackle the supreme task of rebuilding our fatherland. This was our consuming wish." That is right: we must rebuild our fatherland on the foundation of the precious sacrifice you made. We must not allow our fatherland to perish. Following your dying wish we, as one body at our university, must become the core of the nation and vigorously strive to build a new Japan and to create a new culture.

At this auditorium, so full of memories, where you gathered many times, and where a year ago the entire university gathered in this auditorium to bid you all good-bye, we are about to have a memorial service for you: I feel that your spirits have returned to be with us today. We stand in awe of the sacrifice you have made. I trust you would accept our inmost and heartfelt feelings in conducting a memorial service, I humbly preside to conduct this ceremony personally, in the manner suited to a university, without specific religious rituals, and dedicated to your noble souls and to your lives as patriots.

Now, to express my deepest sorrow, I should like to dedicate two elegies to your spirits:

Cherry blossoms are in full bloom,
One cannot but cry for the lives of brave men
Who are now dead.

Although you died in the war,
Your lives will return and
I will protect our country with you.

The souls of my dear university students and staff, please accept our dedication.

Note: This was a *komon* (an official declaration to the gods), read at the memorial ceremony at the University of Tokyo for the students and staff killed in the war. March 30, 1946.

FOREWORD TO THE JAPANESE EDITION

Yutaka Tatsuno

It is heartbreaking for an old man like myself to read the last wills and testaments of young men in the springtime of their lives such as these you find in this collection.

In the war we lost tens of thousands of such students who would now be our close friends. Our homeland is now reduced in size. For the first time in our history we are forced to live without the essentials of life: clothing, food, and housing. Just getting enough to eat on any given day has become an exhausting experience. Great as they are, however, even these difficulties will be gradually overcome over time. All this pales into insignificance, however, when we think of so many young students who left the university never to be seen again. It is painful to find oneself still alive in old age while so many of our young men died. It all seems an unforgivable and unbearable breach of the way things ought to be.

No matter how we look at it, the war was a losing proposition. We were intoxicated by our successful and daring *beau geste* at the very beginning of the war, and it led to a certain complacency and negligence on our part as a nation. For this we were punished by the power of the enemy's technical skills and great wealth, as well as by the very wrath of heaven. It is to deliberately blind oneself to reality to foolishly repeat the Buddhist saying "the wrong cannot beat the right" (or "virtue always triumphs over vice"). Wars are not decided by personal worth or national virtue. Wars are decided by power, and we had no previous experience of such a thing. When we finally became aware, deep in our hearts, of these realities of power, it was already too late. By then so many of our gifted university students had already fallen as casualties of war.

So it is not surprising that tears come to my eyes as I read the collected memories and letters of these fallen students. Their high spirits, their idealism, their bounding young energy can be found on every page and in every line. It was the springtime of their lives. These young Japanese men, while they fought as was their duty, also struggled to set down in writing and pass on to others their many questions, sorrows, and hopes. My heart is heavy and burdened by these writings, but at the same time, I am inspired and refreshed to see that their ideas and feelings were unaffected by the stifling ideologies of military bureaucrats and other ignorant people. They lived and died under vastly different circumstances. Some felt the heat of an oppressive sun, others moved under the pale light of a cool moon. Some scraped along the bottom of the sea in a submarine, others flew in the freedom of the skies. At the time they wrote, all were thinking how lucky they were to still be alive. As they put their thoughts and feelings on paper, some expressed the ideas that had influenced them in their school days. Some looked poetically at a blade of grass or smiled at a hidden flower. While they lay wounded in bed, the hearts of some ached for their sweethearts. And so many wrote messages of farewell to their parents, brothers, and sisters.

What marvelous young men they were. Though we sent them off from the University's gates some years ago, we must keep them ever fresh in our grateful hearts. I beg you, surviving family members, please take up and read from time to time these writings left behind by your fallen young men. I beg you to treasure forever the memory of these noble youth. I beg you never to forget the tragedy that brought all this about. I hope that by our respectful and worthy mourning, our future as a nation will be directed and enlightened. And may the tears that flow from the eyes of our nation help in some way to comfort and ease the burden of loss of those who so tragically lost their loved ones.

TRANSLATOR'S NOTES

1. *Harukanaru Sanga ni* was compiled by the group established by the University of Tokyo Student Government (or, Student Autonomous Society) called the Tōdai Senbotsu Gakusei Shuki Henshū Iinkai (Committee for the Compilation of the Writings of the University of Tokyo Students Killed in the War), and was published by the University of Tokyo Co-Op Publication Department in December 1947. Then, the Nihon Senbotsu Gakusei Shuki Henshū Iinkai (Committee for the Compilation of the Writings of the Japanese University Students Killed in the War) was formed and it took over the task of compiling the more inclusive version, including the fallen students of other universities and colleges, and published *Kike Wadatsumi no Koe* (*Listen to the Voices from the Sea*) which they considered to be the sequel to *Harukanaru Sanga ni* in 1949 and the publication of the latter was ceased. (*Kike Wadatsumi no Koe* contains some pieces or parts of *Harukanaru Sanga ni*.) The University of Tokyo Press, however, published *Harukanaru Sanga ni* in 1951 as the first title in its series, Tōdai Shinsho (the University of Tokyo New Books). Then it was out of print for some time until a newly designed edition, called *shinsō-ban*, was published in 1989. This translation is based on the 1989 edition.

2. English translations of Japanese words are within parentheses. Notes in the Japanese text have also been place within the English text. Translators' longer notations are footnoted when appropriate.

3. A longer row of spaced periods (..........) indicates sections omitted by the original editors.

4. All the dates, when available, have been moved to the beginning of the letters in accordance with the usual English standard. The original letters almost always follow the Japanese custom of placing the dates at the end.

5. In order to avoid unnecessary confusion for the English language reader, the translators resisted the trendy practice currently in vogue in Japan to present Japanese names in English language documents in Japanese style with family name first and the given name next. However, there is one exception to this decision. The

xvii

names in the subheadings at the start of each new student-soldier
section, is presented in accordance with the rules set by the Nihon
Kokugo Shingikai (the Japanese Language Council). The family
name of he person is first, in capital letters, followed by the first
name with the initial letter capitalized.

6.   When the student-soldiers used foreign words, such as German
     words, which they were using in their everyday conversation, they
     are retained here (with English translation) in order to convey the
     scholarly practice of the time.

7.   Throughout the text the reader will find em-dashes used in substi-
     tution in two situations. One, words censored by the military
     authorities, such as troop locations. The other is when the student-
     soldiers omitted names out of respect for privacy for a specific
     person.

—Writings of the University of Tokyo Students—
Killed in World War II

SASAKI, Hachirō

Born March 7, 1922. From the Tokyo metropolis. Having graduated from the First Higher School,[1] he entered Tokyo Imperial
University, Faculty of Economics, in April 1942. Entered the
Navy Corps in 1943. He was killed in action, April 14, 1945, in
the skies over the Okinawa Sea as a member of the Shōwa Special
Attack Unit (one of the Special Attack Corps which later came to
be called "kamikaze pilots.")

"Love," "War," and "Death"
—Relating to *Karasu no Hokuto Shichisei* (*Crows' Seven
Northern Stars* [*or: The Great Dipper*]) by Kenji Miyazawa—

—November 10, 1943. On the occasion of the University
students' being sent off to war—

(A class reunion of the First Higher School's Liberal Arts II
Section was held on November 10th. Hachirō Sasaki read
this essay on that occasion, and it may be considered as his
will, with the theorizing on Kenji Miyazawa as something
of a pretext.)

Kenji Miyazawa is one of the poets I most adore and respect
because of his upbringing, his character, and the personal flair he has
developed. His ideology, something that runs straight through the core

---

[1] Before the Education Reform of 1948, compulsory education covered eight years in
Japan. After the first six years most students passed a competitive examination and
advanced to the academic track of *Chūgakkō* ("middle schools") for boys, *Kōtō-
jogakkō* ("girls' high schools"), or technical schools, most for five years except a limited number for four years in some rural areas. They are junior and senior high schools
today. The next level was the three-year college. Some of those, called *Senmon-gakkō*
(specialized colleges) which included medical schools and engineering colleges, were
for both male and female students. The most academically competitive three year colleges, however, were the *Kōtō-gakkō* (higher schools), which prepared male students
for entrance to the next level, the three-year universities. In order to advance from
higher schools to a university, students had to pass an entrance examination. The most
prestigious university in Japan was Tokyo Imperial University, the alma mater of all
the student-soldiers represented in this volume. Private universities, such as Keio
Gijuku University, had their own *Yoka* (Preparatory Division) instead of a higher
school so the students could advance to the university level without having to take the
entrance examination that those coming from other higher schools or colleges had to
pass in order to be accepted.

of all his works, is most important and touches my heart powerfully. The idea that is summarized in his verse, "unless the entire world becomes happy, there can be no individual happiness," is so right, pure, and sound—a human being's love, as a human being, for beauty —that it is inexpressible in a single sentence. This same ideology, moreover, deep and filled with an oriental fragrance, exactly corresponds to those ideal conceptions of people and of society that have been developing inside me for some time now. Concerning Miyazawa's views on war, I would say that his portrayal of them in the children's story which I have already mentioned, entitled *Karasu no Hokuto Shichisei,* exactly expresses my feelings on the matter. This is the reason for my citing references here to the entire text. I was once given the nickname "Crow." And now I am applying to be a Navy flier. Perhaps there is a certain symmetry even in such silly details; but, at any rate, I shall attempt to write down exactly how my thoughts are running by explicating Miyazawa's views as they are found in the text itself.

Although it is something of a secondary element to the points under present discussion, I cannot say either that at the present time the part involving the Captain and his love, Gunboat, has no connection with my situation—but I shall let that go for now. What touches my heart the most is the scene where the Captain, even while anticipating that he will be killed in an action against the enemy the next day, prays, "I do not know whether or not it is better for me to win this war or for the Mountain Crow to win. It is all according to your wish. I am going to fight as well as I can because fate has decided that so it must be. Everything, absolutely everything, is as you wish."

And another thing about Miyazawa that touches my heart is his deeply human and most beautiful way of thinking with regard to "love," "war," and "death"—a way of thinking that comes across clearly in the passage where, as he was burying the Mountain Crow, he prays: "Oh, Lord Majel (a made-up name of a god he is praying to), please make this world to soon become a place where we do not have to kill an enemy whom we cannot hate. If such a thing were to come about, I would not complain even if my body were torn to pieces many times over." When we face up to issues such as these in our own deepest selves, is there any more human, beautiful, and even sublime way of doing so? And in this whole world is there any other setting wherein one's courage and strength as a human being, in the very truest sense of that term, are so beautifully expressed? So let us not toss this story off lightly by saying, "It is only a tale for children."

The images of "love," "war," and "death," both reflected upon by and reflecting on those who possess genuinely right, pure, and sound hearts, must be exactly so.

Of course, I would never say anything like: "I do not know which is better, to win the war or to lose it." I believe that the advancement of human history can only be achieved when every race and every nation makes its best effort to work for the good and the benefit of the people and for the nation's greater prosperity. I also believe that every nation which finds itself in a war has the obligation of fighting through it with a positive attitude. On the issue of whether we are going to win or lose the war, however, I cannot afford to have an opinion. On the contrary, we theorists who happen to be students of economics have studied what the source of the advancement of world history is, why wars have to happen, what the end results of them might be, and what would be the keys to winning or losing them. By seriously studying problems such as those just described, we came to understand what real productivity is—not just inside a factory or with a single production process, or indeed any productivity that we can see—but the productivity which is involved in that whole entity we call the national economy. Although we should consider this last as a concrete expression of the nation's total strength, we also learned that, at the same time, it is a fateful and inevitable power which transcends all the efforts of our individual idealism. We can no longer be conceited about the power of our individual strength, and neither can we believe that our personal effort is linked to the hope for our nation's victory and for the liberation of all Asian peoples. The only thing we can look forward to is that, from the viewpoint of world history and transcending the position of the individual citizen, our private effort might be conjoined to the nation's in fostering the advancement of that history. I do not want all this to be confused with the philosophy of Hajime Tanabe [a philosopher and professor at the Kyoto Imperial University, 1885–1962], but in these matters we can really and truly—and at one and the same time—be both citizens of the nation and citizens of the world. If we insist on being only Japanese and on maintaining only Japanese positions, then we shall really have to hate our enemies, Great Britain and America. My own attitude, however, is much more humanistic, and something like that of Miyazawa's Crow. This way of looking at things does not require me to hate people whom I do not have to hate.

That is my thinking. In all honesty, those slogans that our military leaders spread around strike me as phrases that may sound good but are basically empty, and which are spread for the sole purpose of inflaming the masses. Also, I always want to be on the side of those people who are in the right, just as I wish to be on the opposite side of those who are essentially either wrong or arrogant—regardless of whether they are the enemy or so-called allies. To us, likes and dislikes, and love and hate as well, are all purely human concerns, and I cannot love or hate someone just because of that person's nationality. Of course it would be quite different in a situation where one is confronted by an antagonist and when neither is able to understand the other because of differences in nationality or ethnicity. I would not wish, however, just because of differences in nationality, to fail to respect something that is in fact noble and beautiful—or to fail to recognize as such things that are ugly and contemptible.

Then why am I volunteering to be "*Umi no Washi*" (Sea Eagle), a naval flier? Right now my feeling about this is that, even though I am Japanese, I am quite detached from any narrow *chauvinism* (narrow-minded and phobic ethnocentrism); therefore, the stance that I must adopt at present is purely that of a human being, just a man, without any reference to nationality. Even though I am not like Carlyle [Thomas Carlyle, 1795–1881], who found himself to be a human being who had been brought into this world without any knowledge of either a father or a mother, I was still more or less accidentally placed in the land of Japan and given into the charge of my father and mother; so I simply wish to fulfill my fate as a student who accepts the responsibilities that have been placed upon him. After careful consideration, my present wish is, with all my might, to live out what is left of my life in accordance with that fate, and with the twin benefits of the academic training I have received and a body that I have disciplined and built up. The way I feel now is that all of us should accept the fates that we were born with, do our best in each's own predetermined way, and fight as hard as we can. It is only being a coward to use foolish excuses in attempts to escape and hide from what our fate has decreed. Let us move forward together along the path that has been laid out for us, and leave it to heaven to decide whether the final outcome will be victory or defeat. I believe that the advancement of world history depends on each one, in his own privately ordained way, doing his very best. Although I am merely a single human being, I wish to live to the end as a human being, through and through, without ever being a coward.

In order to make this world right and better, we are making a pile of stones—one stone at a time. We want to pile the largest and the most stable stones available on the tower that our predecessors built. If we set an unstable stone, it would cause the tower to tumble down, taking with it all those stones piled by others—I would not want to be that sort of stone. I hope that, if possible, our fatherland will play a major role in the new world history; and we have to do our very best to make it possible. With respect to our nation's domestic situation, far too many antiquated customs have not been shaken off and still exist. This situation concerns me a good deal, and it makes me feel that, in themselves, our will to win the war and our determination to persevere until the end are not enough. I would also think it imperative that we take the responsibility upon ourselves both for the structure of society and for productive relations within it, things that must be carried out along rational and scientific lines. In the final analysis, the only thing we can do is to work as hard as we can at whatever assignments are handed to us.—I would say that to hope for anything beyond that would be disrespectful towards the divine.

OI, Hidemitsu

> Born October 2, 1914. Through Toyama Higher School, entered the University, Faculty of Natural Science, Department of Mathematics, in 1934. Graduated in 1937. Entered the barracks, September 1, 1938. Killed in action June 14, 1941, in Shihshuyüan, (Shantung Province,) in northern China.

(To the minister, from the barracks)

Dear Reverend:

Sorry for not having written you for so long.

For the first time in many years, I have been away from the church for the longest time (because I am in the barracks and the Army does not allow me to do so). As I take a good look at myself, I cannot help but notice the negative effect which this has had on me. There have been certain situations wherein maintaining a "Christian softheartedness" has been very difficult indeed. Of course, under the current restrictions on prayer and the Bible, were I to say that there had been no negative effects it would not say much for my spiritual life in the past. Still, however, because I am aware of the changes which have already taken place, I have a powerful hunger for the Bible and the strength which it provides. Even in a busy and constantly changing life such as the one I lead now, in which the word *yorokobi* (joy) is made equivalent to an opportunity for a little rest, its deeper biblical meaning comes through with greater urgency and I feel a keen awareness of what true joy must mean to those who possess it.

Every day my comrades are rushed off to sweat out their training but I, even while undergoing the same training, am daily able to reserve some precious little time for prayer. When we are made to run in full kit and with weapons in our hands, even breathing freely becomes a struggle because the strings of a canteen can choke me. Under these conditions I wind up either being physically beaten or with feelings of depression. In such situations I have tried to say the Lord's Prayer, matching the rhythm of its words to the tempo of our double-time. The actual syllables of the Lord's Prayer do not lend themselves to this, but by inserting a vowel here and there I can both pray and continue to run double-time.

In this way I am able to transcend whatever my eyes might happen to light upon—the sky, clouds, etc.—and become even more conscious of being a servant to our eternal Lord. Especially from this same Lord's Prayer, I am taught even His *chūho* (maintaining harmony between God and man), and so I can well imagine the pains that he suffered. The idea that he lives and works with me fills my heart to the brim with a variety of meanings. —And, in the end, I am able to spend every day in good health and high spirits.

The war stole my life away when it was at its most important point, but I am not going to be finally brought down as a victim of circumstance; rather, I am doing my best to become the sort of man who can overcome war itself by combining the strong spirit of patience with the powerful fighting spirit which my experience in the military has taught me.

My very best to everyone in the group.

In the Lord,

Hidemitsu

(To his mother, April 17, 1940)

My Dear Mother:
    The day of departure has finally arrived.

But I am going away in high spirits and good health; so, please take really good care of yourself and I pray that, when I return home after all the hardships that probably lie ahead, I'll be able to see you in even better health than now.

I am trying to act as though I haven't a care in the world and am perfectly balanced emotionally, but the truth is that I leave for battle amid many unsettled matters. That is, there are these feelings of emptiness and loneliness which accompany those of sadness at having to leave loved ones behind. I believe that I have prepared myself and am ready to head in the direction of serious danger, as I am fully confident in God's invisible but providential control of the situation. This is why I wanted all of you—Mother, Yoshimitsu, and Mieko—to understand my frame of mind and, because you understood, to send me off with at least a smile; but apparently the love between a parent and a child is far too deep and poignant for that. I do not mind your tears, Mother, but I beg you please to spend each day from now on in a cheerful mood, at least as much as you can, and in anticipation of the letters I will be writing. If I were to leave home with only tears for a farewell, I might feel that I was headed less surely for battle than for death. So, I really wish you would think of my going as though I were only leaving home with fishing gear and a sketch book. Please promise me that you are determined never to shed any more tears.

The beauty of the cherry blossoms and of the genial spring sun helped to put me in a tranquil mood and, as I reexamined what is in my heart, a variety of new emotions rose up. In the past we used to talk about the joys and pains of life and other complex subjects with a great confidence, assuming that we understood one another so well—or indeed I thought that I fully comprehended: but, now it seems clear that almost all of that was nothing, but matters in the process of passing. I feel that salvation through Christ, and through Christ alone, is the only bridge of hope left for us linking (our indifferent world) to the unchanging world. What I suppose I am saying is that, even though my faith is itself not unshakable, it is by comparison far stronger than anything else in this world.

It must seem truly astonishing that a person such as myself, who in the past so truly hated and feared anything connected with war, can now concentrate so fully—to the absolute exclusion of all other thoughts, emotions, etc.,—on learning everything there is to learn about preparing for war. But however startling a phenomenon this might seem to, say, a member of my family, to the person who is right in the middle of all this—i.e., to me—the situation seems more than natural. It is possible that someone, and sadly, might pose a question: "Are you then getting to be a soldier so completely?" The only possible answer I could give, in the interests of accuracy, would be a qualifying one: "Not really, but I am placed in the role of a soldier and going through a special training to function as a soldier." That is, I have not become a soldier "through and through."

What so far is the most painful and depressing aspect of my life in the military involves certain misgivings about the state of my emotions—gnawing doubts about what I have always considered very fine and keen emotions. What I am worried about is whether or not they may be deteriorating to such a point that I may no longer be able either to be afraid of anything or to react to anything. I have even felt the urge to assume a fighting stance more or less automatically, while at the same time remaining as a person with permanently keen emotions, instead of being reduced gradually to a beast. Still and all, I am certain that I would not commit an unreasonable act. It is possible that I might be taken off guard momentarily but I am confident that, given time, I'll move toward the final victory in the best way I can possibly manage. At this point, of course, I have no idea as to whether or not that final victory will cost me my life. Because of that, I can leave home cheerfully. So, I ask you, who are remaining at home, to lead peaceful and pleasant lives and watch over me as I am going through my training as if my life (death!) depends on it. Just as my death would be the Lord's will and therefore no cause for tears, so too even my survival should not be cause for any premature celebration—because it would not necessarily mean final victory.

Looking back over what I have written, it seems a rather long, gloomy report—but please read only my smile. From now on I intend to write you about much more interesting things, and lots of humorous and pleasant ones too.

I haven't written all that much lately, and for a while there I thought that my head might have turned to stone; but I realize now that I am still able to write, able in fact to write a good deal, and also, as something of a bonus, that human feelings are gushing out of me just as they do from ordinary people. So I'll be writing you now and then about what I am thinking and feeling, and I hope that, on the receiving end, the letter will provide food for pleasant conversation. With this I close my first letter.

Hidemitsu

(A letter to a minister)

Dear Reverend:

With prayers for God's blessings.

Please be assured that, thanks to God's grace, I am well. I feel very fortunate that, even in this war zone, I can quietly praise God with a hymn in the quiet of the evening. I can say that my present situation is filled with God's grace. I cannot do anything about the constant threat to my very existence, because after all this *is* a war zone, but my peace of mind allows me to put up with things much more easily.

I entered a Chinese church for the first time this evening. It looked as though a prayer meeting was going on, so I stopped in on my way back from an inspection tour of the town. Middle-aged men and women and some older people were gathering. When I told them that I was a Japanese Christian they seemed very pleased; and with happy faces, they told me that they had a Japanese Bible and went out of their way to produce it. I think they did so because I was looking at a Chinese Bible with curiosity. I did not stay very long but was greatly pleased when, just before I took my departure, an old man tried to present me with a book, *Shutsu Ejiputo Ki* (*The Exodus*). I thought it was so nice. Walking back through the town, although this village was burned to the ground, I realized in my heart that the village was so filled with the joy of believers.

I am full of thoughts for the church and praying for God's grace. Regards to everyone.

In the Lord,
Hidemitsu

(A letter to his mother, October 1940)

October 12, 10:00 p.m.
My Dear Mother:

By joining the military I have really come to learn a lot about patience. We have often heard it said that the truly courageous man is less prone to anger, but I think, at least to a certain extent, that it may really be true in my case. I cannot say that there is no emotional distress, but since I always keep myself in good physical shape I am very happy to find myself upbeat and spiritually healthy as well, so much so that I feel able, every day, to continue to do my best. From now until March of next year I shall be helping to train the recruits, and so I shall be very busy indeed; however, since I am physically strong enough for certification, I will do my best to train them well, and train them to be good *chūtai* (company) soldiers.

Now that the cold weather is upon us, I pray that Yoshimitsu will not work too hard for his health's sake, and also that Mieko will soon be able to leave her bed. Though I dropped a postcard to Mieko just the other day, I have since dreamt a dream which, perhaps even beyond reasonable expectations, fills me with hope for her.

Please take good care of yourself too, Mama. And be particularly careful not to overextend yourself time and again. Keeping that caution in mind, then, I think it would be a fine thing to maintain a positive state of mind by taking up something like sunbathing.—I am so grateful to Yone (a maid), who seems to be doing such a good job for all of you. She and the maid at my older sister's house both deserve "medals of merit," don't you think? I do, and please tell them so. The only regrettable thing in connection with these women is that their husbands who are in the military might not be doing as good a job, to receive medals in the battlefield they hope for, as they themselves are at home.

I think I have already mentioned that I do not need any winter clothing. So please do not ever worry about that; I have never yet had a single night when the cold kept me from sleeping. I remember feeling cold once during a night march, but that was the only time. During rest stops it is quite warm sleeping in the straw, even though it does not compare to sleeping in *futon*. But straw makes rustling noises when one tosses about in it, and at time*s I* feel as though I had descended into John's world (John was his dog). —There are even moments when I feel that John is right here next to me, even though this is an unknown little town in northern China. Actually, it is Lieutenant Kakutani, our information officer, not John, who is sleeping there; so once, in the middle of the night (doubtless due to this outrageous and even insolent imagination of mine), I all of a sudden had to break out into a smile.

I have also had a very interesting lesson about controlling my feelings—more accurately, my sentiments—when I learned that taking long walks by myself would, only momentarily, but really without any reason, bring on feelings of depression. On such occasions I have a little dialogue with myself which goes something like this:

"What is bothering you?"
"Nothing is bothering me."

Then:
"Why are you depressed?"
"I have no idea."

I think that what it all boils down to is a simple matter of fatigue, but when I am in the middle of one of these moods it feels as though one side of myself is fighting with another side—one "I" is trying hard to cheer myself up: the other "I" refuses to be cheered. I think that through this process my heart is being trained to be strong.

It just so happens that I have run out of stationery, so I will write again soon. Good night. Good-bye. I am going to bed now.

Hidemitsu

(A letter to his younger sister)

My Dear Sister:

Is it getting colder in Tokyo? Or perhaps, I wonder, it might not be quite cold yet, and may rather be the most comfortable season of the year. When autumn arrives in Toyama we have to get ourselves psychologically ready—as though to say, "It (winter) is sure to come now"—for the inevitable arrival of winter's snow and low temperatures.

But if we here feel very sad and lonely about autumn's passing, autumn in Tokyo is quite different, isn't it? Do you understand what I mean? Speaking for myself, it may be true that this is my first autumn in northern China, but it brings me great happiness to at least realize that I have the objectivity to enjoy it and to feel its good qualities. I hope you will take my word for it that an autumn in northern China is not bad at all. The night stars are the same as in Japan and, as with so many other things, I am attracted by their beauty because they remind me of home.

Still, Japan itself is most certainly the best place to be, and Tokyo is the best of the best. Even more particularly than that, our home in Setagaya is indeed the finest place of all. No matter how nice northern China may be, there is nothing more beautiful or lovable than the most beautiful thing in Japan—my home. Neither is even the fine quality of autumn in northern China at all comparable to the beauty of those Tokyo autumns, which we so quietly enjoyed together—two brothers and a sister, with our mother in the center.

At any rate, I am going through my training everyday in nature's preciously clean and beautiful air, and I cannot help but get stronger. Warmest regards to everyone.

In the Lord,
Your older brother

Dear autumn wind: Please be gentle,
for my beloved mother is sick in bed in this house.

"On *Karen*"[1]

We often hear of the sentiment called "*karen*," and I have often experienced that feeling myself. To feel empathy over someone who is tiny, small, or weak, is indeed one of the most desirable of the numerous natural sentiments we feel as human beings. Weakness in itself—if someone, e.g., is weak and has no one to rely upon but is lacking in substance himself—would not, I would think, cause us to feel any sense of *karen*. It seems that this sentiment is only roused within us at the sight of someone who is not strong and who still manages to maintain a sense of him-/herself, who somehow, and despite obvious shortcomings, continues to give his/her best effort. When the weak expect the strong to protect them, then all it amounts to in the end is a lack of moral courage, and no sentiment of "*karen*" would be involved.

As a commander I am quite often powerfully moved whenever I see a soldier who, lacking in natural ability, but supported by the sheer emotion of being sent off with Japanese Hinomaru (the Rising Sun) flags, tries his very hardest to come through even though the outcome might not be the best possible. The feeling sparked by such a situation is the emotion we call "*karen*."

I feel the same way when I see soldiers, with hands that are caked with dirt because of the long stretch of time between opportunities to take baths, trying as best they can to clean their weapons. They carry on with hands terribly swollen by frigid temperatures, and with rough-knuckled fingers that seem to be difficult for them even to bend. —But still they carry on.

---

[1] A term meaning pretty, lovely, cute, sweet, pitiful, and carrying a tender sentiment, complete with sympathy and affection, towards the person to whom it is applied.

I get that same sense of *karen* and am also deeply moved when I see a soldier single-mindedly trying his hardest even though his efforts might be in vain, despite the fact that he has already been put down as no good by his superior officer. These men have to have a world of their own, a place where they can show themselves off with pride. At the very least, they must have a loving father, mother, or siblings. No matter how sincere and genuine they are, they may receive a poor evaluation just because of their low talent level; they may even be nagged about unsatisfactory performance in various exercises. Even though they possess precious and jewel-like hearts, and even though their fathers, mothers, and siblings are hoping for the best for them and expecting so much from them, in the long run the Army treats them as feeble and powerless. Every time I come upon such a case, I experience the strongest possible emotion—*karen*—and feel so much for each of these soldiers.

I once experienced the feeling of *karen* in connection with prostitutes. They are utterly powerless, and yet they make desperate efforts to survive. The large majority of these women work with demonic fervor to make themselves attractive to men, and attempt to entice them with their sleeves all rolled up. These therefore cannot possibly be objects for the feeling of *karen,* simply because the force of their personalities is so strong—perhaps even stronger than men's. On the other hand, there may be a few prostitutes who are truly *karen,* and nothing makes them so more than those moments of "epiphany" when these particular women are awakened, even slightly, to the consciousness that ideas such as *shūyō* (moral training) or about *zen* (good) even exist. When those moments occur they are usually totally broken people but, even though they are weak and desperate, they continue to try very hard. These are the type of women who come as far as northern China. —They may be the brave ones in the front lines of overseas expansion, but I still wonder what in the world they are trying to accomplish.

Another occasion when I was deeply filled with the emotion of "*karen*" was one time when I saw a Chinese man and his child. The man was about forty years of age, tall, heavy-bodied, oval-faced, and with full cheeks. He did not look particularly affluent, but neither did he appear to be as poor and dirty as those on the lowest rung of the ladder. He was standing still by the side of the road and watching the triumphant Imperial Japanese Army as they marched through. He was holding a small child of about four in his arms. Both of them, man and child, were after all citizens of a defeated nation, and I wondered how the strutting soldiers appeared to them and what their thoughts were. There was no sign of servility in their faces, and in fact, I thought that I saw China's future possibilities hidden in them—especially in the face of the child who was being protected by the defeated grownup. In spite of all that, they were not even glanced at; rather, they were being left behind in that cold village so far distant from civilization. While I went on marching, my heart felt as though it had been torn out by the sight of those two *karen* people.

I also know a young and *karen* maiden. As is not unusual with humankind, she once had both youth's beauty and the joy of falling in love. Things being the way they are in this world, however, her dreams went unfulfilled and had to be set aside. She finds herself left behind and all alone, yet because of her constant and sincere disposition a little glow always emanates from her gentle face. Although she has no great future prospects, she contrives to fill each of what would otherwise have been empty days either by sewing or offering volunteer service at Kokubō Fujinkai (Women's Society for National Defense), or often enough doing her best to make her work effective by rubbing hands which have become benumbed with cold. Whenever I see her in such situations I cannot help but want to pray to Him to pity her. Even from the very earliest time we see evidence that the sentiment of *karen* grows stronger when there is a touch of sadness involved; in the *final* analysis, anything which can truly be called beautiful must include some such admixture.

Finally, I find that I must write something about my own sense of *karen*. I am often far from forthright, and although I strive to be a man of ideals I am still basically a weak person. I know all about the importance of being earnest and of maintaining a high degree of seriousness but, at the same time, I am also aware of the built-in weaknesses to these qualities. Others may not know about my own weaknesses. They would not be aware of my inner frailty, which is in inverse proportion to my outer toughness.

I think I can say, however, that I am the world's greatest authority on myself, and can clearly distinguish the inside from the outside. I know that indeed I do have at least the hope of feeling *karen* for myself precisely because I see so clearly how hard at least a part of me is trying to do its best. —I shudder at merely the thought of my lively personality being dwindled down to *donchō* (being dull and cautious), and my *ganko* (stubbornness) reduced to simple servility. Although I find

myself in a very difficult position—in a straitjacket, you might say—
I shall still continue to do my very best; moreover, now that things
have developed as they have, I will be turning to prayer—for I firmly
believe in His gracious protection.

Oh, what a *karen* person am I!

November 27, 1940

MEGURO, Akira

> Born November 10, 1916. Through the Second Higher School,
> entered the University, Faculty of Letters, Department of
> Sociology, in April 1937. Entered the barracks in March 1941.
> Died in September 1941, in a military field hospital in Yüehchou,
> central China, of an illness contracted on the battlefield.

(A letter to his father)

September 16, 1941
Dear Father:

Father, autumn is here. I was startled by the cool autumn wind
after suffering from the well-over one hundred degree temperatures
we've been experiencing until now. The skies are beautiful too and are
filled with stars. Insects are singing around us. In this alien land of
China any insects—whether they are *kōrogi* (crickets) or *matsumushi*
(*Madasumma marmorata*, a kind of cricket), or just about any type of
autumn insect that we used to hear in Japan—make us soldiers feel
nostalgic about home. So, whenever we get together and talk, our con-
versations are always limited to the mountains and rivers of home, and
also to the food we enjoyed at home.

Father, our Yamamori Squad is now in Hankou (major city in
Hupeh Province). Our several months' training in that severe summer
heat will now be tested, we hope successfully, during this autumn season. On September 9th, the day of the Chrysanthemum Festival, our
unit completed preparations for moving out to what was announced as
our next station. That is the town of Tangyang, which is some 350 kilometers beyond Hankou. It was 10 o'clock in the morning when our
automobiles left in the quiet autumn rain, headed for a place which was
to be my very first battlefield. Our automobile detachment unit of a
few dozen vehicles moved forward over gentle, undulating hills, one

following another. At times we could not move because the tires became mired in incredibly muddy places; or at other times, all together and with enormous effort, we pulled vehicles up hills they could not have climbed otherwise. Other vehicles broke down completely. But after four days of traveling and innumerable hardships, our unit finally arrived here at Hankou at 10 o'clock in the evening on the 12th. It turns out that we are now about to embark on a ship, and with no idea of our destination. In any event, we really have no other choice than that of continuing to follow the imperial orders.

So as it finally turns out, Father, the path that I will be traveling as a soldier in this unprecedented war—referred to as the "China Incident"—had already been decided on. The inevitable day is finally here. You have many times urged me to prepare mentally for living each day as it comes, and every time you did I gathered a new courage and planned out how, no matter how difficult the situation, to follow your advice. I regret to say though that, from a spiritual standpoint, I am not yet fully motivated. All I can do is just go on with a young man's spirit of *mōmetsu-hō* (the law of blind destruction).

Honestly, dear Father, there have been so many occasions when I wanted to appeal to you and confide in you and mother as intimately as I did in the days of childhood. Perhaps these feelings were like those of a young bully who goes home to his parents to confess what he has done. . . . There were so many times when I wished so very much I could have you hear me out about so many things—times when I felt so alone and lonely that at night I just went out quietly to look at the starry skies.

Sometimes I even felt jaundiced and sorry for myself, thinking that the only place where I could possibly live would be in a kind and gentle place and amid the company of the tranquil souls whom I longed for. But I believe that even this sort of bad dream will be blown away once I face my first battle. More importantly, I have learned thoroughly that soldiers fight not so much by tolerating hardships as by utterly disregarding whatever hardships and pain they must endure. It makes me feel good to think that I too will not be defeated by any foreseeable hardships. Under no circumstances, Father, shall I ever act in a cowardly manner; so long as I live I shall continue to move forward. The amulet that you so kindly sent me the other day is not meant for clinging to life, but it would make even a weak soldier a courageous one. The more I reflect upon your kindest thoughts and deepest love, Father and Mother, with which this amulet is filled, the more determined am I than ever to be strong.

And so I feel fully prepared, body and soul, and at this point in time there is nothing left for me to do but to move on to fight in the war as a strong and courageous soldier. I have prepared for this challenge in the same manner as those *samurai* of long ago, who were born to face death so honorably, with such good grace, and without any regrets. Just as you have always taught me to do, Father, I have carefully planned out just how to campaign here as a righteous and strong soldier. —And, Father, that is not all; I have also bid a quiet farewell to all the people I have known for a long time.

Beloved parents, I cannot find words to express anything close to adequate appreciation for what you, Father and Mother, have done for me. Father, the house and home, which by your own hard work you built from nothing, will always be a beloved memory. I find it truly hard to believe that such a beautiful home, a little world so filled with perfect harmony, could ever exist on this earth. That was a piece of fine art that you created. In it we children were brought up so lovingly. There was never anything lacking or wanting—I remember the warm steam that surrounded us at dinnertime. Ever since I arrived here what I have thought and meditated constantly about is the object of art that you created, Father. The fact that through you I was given the opportunity to see that beautiful harmony is enough to have made my life worth living. Father, your love has been so deep and I have received so much from you for such a long time. Your heart was such a deep loving heart. At this moment of time, please do not worry, and just think of me as doing the best job I possibly can. Now, I must go. The autumn wind is freshening a bit now, and it's wrinkling the moving water of the creek beneath the railroad embankment. I can imagine what a beautiful autumn must have arrived at home, Sendai, by now. This brings back those days in the much cherished past, which I could write about endlessly if I ever once started. So you must excuse me if I end this letter right now for today. Please think of me as I shall always be talking with you.

September 17, 1941
Dear Father:

I am writing you again simply because I have another opportunity to do so and want to take advantage of it. Who knows how much time there will be to write once we begin fighting and will be so by night and day? But what is important, dear Father, is that I have so many more things to tell you than it is possible to write down.

On the —day of March, we left that —*chikkō* (harbor construction) during the course of a storm. A phonograph was playing a march very loudly, and we stood in line on the deck to acknowledge the civilians' farewell greetings. Our ship moved as smoothly as though it were sliding over the Seto Inland Sea, and very late the next afternoon we reached a point where we could see the city lights of Shimonoseki and Moji. That was our point of departure from the *naichi* (mainland Japan).

Genkai Strait was quite rough, but I did not throw up or come close to it even once. When I saw the lights of Wusung early in the morning we were already in Yangtzĕchiang (the Yangtze River). This river was so vast that it could have been an ocean, river, lake, or all of them in one. And so we were on a new continent just like that. Chinese junks were coming and going in the same way they must have been through ages past, and the whole look of the continent was something completely new to us.

We arrived at Nanking on —day of —month. And we spent about a week at —Battalion's barracks here. It was located at the bottom of Lion Mountain, where some stubborn remains of gun-emplacements showed through. Hawks were wheeling around the sky as though they were dancing. I was seeing the Chinese people for the first time personally, and what really left a strong impression were the masses of coolies. When we were ready to disembark from the ship, there were hundreds of them squirming around on the landing pier. They were all wearing rags so tattered that they defy description. There were old ones and young ones alike, all barefooted and walking this way and that way. They left an even stronger impression on me than had the numerous burned houses that I caught glimpses of on our way to the barracks. Things that will not be easy to forget are the scenes at Hsing-chung Mien. In the very early morning, masses of coolies go into the castle there with empty tin cans on their hips, and then in the evenings they come out again through the gate.

On the —day of the —month came the opportunity to move on, and we wound up at Sochiang of the Yangtze River again. As was only to have been expected, the river narrowed on both sides and, every day, the scenes along both banks were the same: hills of reddish earth color, wheat fields, willows, and junks. We arrived at Hankou on the evening of the —month, where we spent a night; we disembarked on the —day, and on the —day we at last began the trip to our final destination, —. It was in Hankou I learned definitely that our military unit was a *jidōsha-tai* (motor car corps) and that —(number) of vehicles were waiting to transport us some 350 kilometers. After bumping along about two days in the cargo sections—it was the evening of the —day of the —month, we reached our destination *butai* (military unit).

Strung across the midsection of a mildly sloping hill with the Tanshui River (said to be a tributary of the Yangtze River) at its back, our post lies within a naturally beautiful setting. In the mornings we are awakened by mountain pigeons and are surprised to hear the braying of donkeys. The earlier fighting had already turned most of this place into ruins, so our residence was just something that was thrown together from Chinese houses. There are many inconveniences but, considering the fact that this is China, the water is clean.

We first-year soldiers were pushed very hard in order to become fully trained; while our seniors were busy on a daily basis transporting war supplies by motor vehicles to a faraway place named —. As summer arrived the color of the leaves turned from light green to a darker shade, frogs grew more and more noisy, and the heat rose to over 100 degrees. Then, just shortly afterwards, or so it seemed, the hum of autumn insects increased, which means that already —months have passed.

As to —, Father, there are so many things I wanted to write you about, such as the shape of the place, the scenery, etc. The only reason I have not mentioned those things is because they verge upon being military secrets, but I would like you to think of this place as I've already described it: I am stationed at an advanced post of the Japanese Army *heitan kichi* (base for war supplies), located in a place of great natural beauty deep inside China. Our soldiers are risking bad roads, and making their runs in beaten-up motor vehicles, choking in dust, all day and all night. Since there are so many problems with mechanical breakdowns, we spend every night and the wee hours of every morning repairing them and getting them ready to go. This is the way in which our days and nights melt into one another.

Father, as I mature in this sort of life and am finally fully trained, I will now be moving on to actual military operations. As I told you yesterday, I am already prepared mentally. Today, I just wanted to let you know how and in what sort of a place I have been soldiering.

The ship anchored as evening was settling in. Now it is already past the time for putting lights out, and it has become very quiet indeed. Even inside the ship some insects are singing, and I hear that we finally will be disembarking at that famous —port tomorrow.

It is already ten o'clock. I have put in another good day of healthy service. I imagine that you are now in a deep sleep, Father, but that since she is such a night owl Mother might still be up. The lights on the second floor are probably still lit at home because both Tai and Shin are such good students, and I can even imagine that dear little Mitchan is still up because of her homework from sewing class.

Goodnight then, everybody, and I hope that I will dream another nice dream tonight.

IWATA, Yuzuru

Born December 2, 1919. Through the Third Higher School, he entered Kyoto Imperial University in April 1941, and entered the Tokyo Imperial University, Faculty of Belles Lettres, Department of French Literature, April 1942. Entered the barracks, April 1943. Died of illness contracted while in service at the Burma Patient Collection Center, August 12, 1944.

– Diary –

April 12, 1943

Standing as we are at this most difficult crossroads in our nation's history, it is quite impossible to find words to describe the corruption, under General Tōjō, of the military officialdom responsible for pointing out the correct course of action. These men are facing the current crisis all but completely ensnared by their shady financial and political connections. I fully realize that their idiotic and slipshod policies with regard to the South Pacific are so haphazard that they are hardly worth discussion. However, we may not be able to expect any really substantial change even if some new cabinet should turn up to replace Tōjō's. Ah, whatever has happened to our loyal and decent citizens? The deterioration of moral standards could hardly go much further, and I myself—an insignificant nobody without official position—am powerless to do anything about it. Now all that I can do is to hold back my tears, swear my utmost loyalty, and prepare to become a *suteishi* (sacrificial stone) for the benefit of the next generation.

April 16, 1943

I went to say good-bye to Prof. Ibuki. He gave me his copy of *Les Cent Meilleurs Poemes*, which he had always kept in his pocket and read with pleasure ever since he purchased it in Paris. I also went to the First Prefectural Middle School.[1]

April 19, 1943

Miss — came to see me. For the first time I thought that I could understand her feelings clearly, but as things are I must remain silent and simply leave for the war. To go to war means exactly to face certain death. In the evening I had a modest farewell party with Sakamoto, Yaguchi, Fukutomi, and Yoshioka. Keenly did I feel in my heart what that renowned loyal subject, Masashige Kusunoki, meant what he said he wished that he could live seven lives in the service of his country (i.e., in fighting for his emperor even as he was facing certain death in a losing war).

– Will –

November 2, 1943

Returned for an overnight stay, and the time has finally come when I will most likely be sent to the front—*isshi hōkō* (sacrificing one's own life for one's people). I shall simply go to war and face death for the sake of my country, saying "*banzai*" to the emperor and praying that my dear fatherland will remain safe forever.

Dear Father: I apologize to you for not having done anything in the area of filial piety. So that I might at least partially make up for this, please accept my death on the battlefield as a child of the emperor.

Dear mother, younger sisters, and everyone in the family: Please stay happy and in good health.

To my dear best friends: I think you know what is in my mind better than anyone else, and I also think you would agree that I am going in the right direction. After I am gone, please think of me and of what I intend to do in the best possible light.

[1] The old-system middle schools extended over five-year periods. For girls, the same level was referred to as "girls' high school." Beginning with the education reform during the Allied Occupation, this level became middle schools and high schools, three years each, most often combined. Additionally, all public schools became coeducational.

To all of those dear acquaintances of mine and compatriots to whom I am unable to write individually: strangely enough—and I really do think that it is a strange thing indeed—no special emotion has come bubbling up even as I am on the point of departure for the war. Even though this might be the last time I can be with my father, mother, and sisters, all I can think about is wanting to eat *botamochi* (a Japanese sweet) and *zenzai* (a thick, azwki-bean sweet soup). Do you not think it strange that such a bottomless optimism resides within the human spirit? —Oh well, everyone, please stay well.

KIKUYAMA, Hiroo

> Born September 6, 1921. From the Third Higher School, he entered the University, Faculty of Jurisprudence, October 1941. Conscripted, December 1943. Killed in action at Echague Airport, Ipeal village on the island of Luzon in the Philippines, April 29, 1945.

– Diary –

October 11, 1943

Why in the world am I taking up arms for the emperor? Or, am I doing it for ideological reasons connected with the motherland, or because of the love which I unquestionably bear towards my parents, or even for the pure natural beauty of the mountains and rivers of Japan that was always my *furusato* (hometown)? Am I about to fight for all of these things, or just a part of them? —Anyway, I have not, at least just at present, gotten around to answering the question of why I should have to risk my life. If things could only be as they were two years ago, when I was so terrified at the thought of death that I kept getting up in the middle of the night to check my face in the mirror for a death shadow. Then again, when I had happily chosen the path of martyrdom as my only means of escape, I would have been glad to board a plane or climb into a submarine just to throw my life away. Now, however, I share the feeling of that elderly author [Tōson Shimazaki, 1872–1943], who recently passed away, saying that "even though I am in my present condition, I still wish somehow to keep on living." So how can I arm myself and go off to fight a war on some distant battlefield? As I turn off the light I peer out from a window of this room at a clear 13th-day moon. Watching the white, snow-like cloud of the night, my psychological readiness during an earlier period to hop into a fighter plane seems dreamlike indeed.

I firmly believe that the basic rule of morality is to be honest with one's own heart. It has to be a case of "pretending to be bad," if not one of downright hypocrisy, for a person who really wishes to survive to man a warplane at the very same time—particularly a plane that carries a high casualty rate with it. The obligation to go into battle is excusable whenever having to do so is a question of one's fate; (of course this fact itself is the problem and also most important, . . .) but to choose to join the army or navy or to fly a warplane is something that requires an individual's own conscious and cold-blooded decision. Any such determination is not to be imposed upon another human being, or made even for oneself on the basis of temporary excitement.

How could I, who have witnessed such foolish and even contemptible behavior among my many friends and acquaintances—and even in myself as well—throw my life away just for the benefit of a few of those friends who are still around whom I respect, as well as for one professor whom I hold in high esteem? This is especially the case since they too are in no way desirous of my death. The best and most understandable reason has to be—is—I, myself. As I take pen in my hand to review the situation, this way of thinking which I have settled on seems inevitable. If this is indeed the case, however, then death itself does not seem to have a clear definition. Sometimes I think that it is all just a matter of fate.

What is the essence of the beauty which is sought after by a haunted genius, the kind that resonates from Beethoven's *Appassionata*? Perhaps it is bound up with the fate of this pitiful human race, which holds up ideals that can never be realized! It might even be that the yearning to create something so superb is involved—though in some hidden, subjective way—in this whole notion that we have to fight a war. And, if such is indeed the case, then nothing remains to be done except to follow the will of the god of fate. I tend to think that Rilke [Rainer Maria Rilke, Austrian poet, 1875–1926] emerges this philosophy. Oh, somehow, now I must face myself as frankly as possible. I have been putting off having to think things completely through, but now the time has finally arrived. I feel impatient! However, I want to try and think calmly.

October 20

I want to write about what happened yesterday. I paid a visit in the

afternoon to the grave of my friend, Taguchi, at Tama cemetery. I
arrived there at 4:30 p.m. But, no matter how hard I tried, I could not
find his grave. I looked everywhere, inspecting tombstones one by
one, until finally I even lost track of where I was and even wound up
once at the edge of a highway. I became so desperate that I even called
his name out loud—"Taguchi!" Still I could not find his tombstone. I
felt as though I would be letting him down if I could not pay my
respects at his gravesite, especially on the last day before my departure
from Tokyo, so I kept on searching for his grave even though it was
getting darker all the time and there was no one else around. I picked
up a book and some flowers that I had left at a well, and had just about
decided on giving up and leaving the place—and, possibly, on returning some other time. Then I found that I still could not give up, and
once again walked around in an unsuccessful search for his grave.
Finally, and just as I was about to abandon my project once and for all,
I happened to glance at the tombstone just behind me—it was
Taguchi's grave. I was delirious. I talked to him out loud. I even had
the illusion that his tombstone moved. By the time I got some fresh
water and put flowers and incense sticks by the gravesite, it had
become so dark that I could barely read the letters on tombstones.
What happened was not just good luck. I cannot explain it in any way
except that Taguchi called me. To a certain extent I do believe in the
existence of spirits. And I told Taguchi that even though I was going
off to war I would not be killed in action. I told him that of course I
would have to risk my life, but would live to get over his death and to
carry on. Perhaps I am slightly exaggerating, but it just might be that
the thought of death has not yet taken a realistic shape in my mind.
The only really important truth may be the very thought of not wanting to die. As Rilke wrote, a loved one who has passed away will live
on in the memory of a living person. Taguchi is alive in my heart, in
Masahisa's, and probably in Iwamiya's heart as well. When I think
about my own death I wonder who, outside of my parents, would take
a similar attitude—and I feel a bit lonesome. However, even if there
were only someone who would just believe that in me there had existed an earnest dedication to life, I think that would be more precious
than anything else. To live as earnestly as one can—there is nothing
else that really matters.

October 22, 1943, morning   At Kamikōchi
    I have a certain feeling that I am writing this note for the benefit

of only one very special person. But I wonder where that one person is —perhaps at the end of the world!

April 25, 1944   (After entering the barracks)

I am going to write this during what free time I have today. Since I am afraid that I may not have an opportunity to see you again, I would like to spend more time and to be as perfect as possible with each word and each letter, but I am not given that time. So I will just have to write as much as possible of what I had planned. I would at least like to have the form and sequence of what I write to be correct, but there is no time to make it so. So here I'll have to be content with putting down whatever comes to mind.

I shall try to write down what has gone on since December 1, the day when you and I, though in different places, first put on a military uniform. I do not know about you, but lately I have begun to wonder how it came to be that I arrived here so lightheartedly, because that was really a strange attitude to take. Of course you could simply say that it was all due to the fact that we came here in such a serene state of mind, but I still think that on that first day there should have been some very serious considerations to mull over—on that day when my fate had already become so definite. But whatever may be the truth about the gravity of the situation on that day, I have the feeling that, even if we should have to face a graver one we would be able to handle the challenge without any problems, and, so long as we were given the proper orders, without losing our poise.

We were the only recruits, so it was only natural that we had to work hard, but an unduly harsh round of duties within the barracks began almost immediately. From the moment when I kicked off the covers and got up in the morning until the lights were turned off at night—there was nothing in the barracks that could not be used as an excuse for being reprimanded except during military training outside in the bitter cold. At times we were forced to remain standing in a corner of our squad room even after the lights had been turned off. As a result of all this we even welcome the outside military training—no matter how cold and difficult it is—where at least we can smoke cigarettes openly, and there are not so many occasions for being knocked around physically.

While on the matter of physical punishment, it might be noted that by the end of December and in early January we were regularly beaten with *jōka* (the leather slippers that are worn inside the barracks) and with leather belts. There were some who were made to stand up for two hours and then brutally beaten and kicked senseless because, our seniors said, the serving of rice was too slow. As you know so well, I am not clever and neither am I quick with regard to physical activity; so, obviously, I was not excepted from the sort of treatment I have just described. They say that the bugle-call which signals lights out carries this message: "Oh, you poor recruits!—You will be going to bed in tears again." And as a matter of fact, I often did have to cry myself to sleep in an "envelope" (i.e., bed) after having been beaten a number of times and shoved into bed. I wept not because of the pain but, rather, because of those feelings of outrage and indignity which I had to endure. It seems that my morale was completely undermined. It is called "five-month training," but I kept computing how many more days still remained out of those five months, and I continued counting down just about every single day. I would look at a cold moon on my way to the toilet at night and keep thinking about how many more full moons I would be seeing from there. I claimed that I wanted to go to the front, because soon it was more a case of "*nakigoto*" (whining a gripe) than anything else. I recall having written you about this "*nakigoto*" of mine around that time and, if I remember correctly, getting a rather stern letter from you in reply. You told me in your letter to "trust in the healing power of time and be strong," and that was very close to the same advice I had been giving myself.—But under the circumstances which prevailed at that particular time, nothing but "*nakigoto*" was really possible.

I could not really feel anything even when I learned of the *gyoku-sai* (lit. meaning is the shattering of a precious stone, and the literal reference is to death with honor, but in practice the term was used in connection with battles in which everyone was killed) of Makin and Tarawa (the Japanese garrisons on both these islands were completely annihilated in November of 1943) or sending off regiment after regiment of soldiers to the battlefront. I naturally wondered how I could go on with this kind of life. Even though I understood how it had come about I could not fully accept it, and therefore, at least subconsciously, I went about criticizing the war, the nation itself, and other important things. I am all but certain that my general attitude was detectable in my letters to you.

Since I am writing this in such haste, I hope that it has somehow come together as something like an accurate record. Even though there were so many things that I was thinking and wanted to write about. . . .

To tell you the truth, what I had most wanted to write about were the people I came into contact with hereabouts. There is no time, however, to write about each person in anything like detail; and, anyway, I lack the confidence to write about what I wanted to.

I don't remember exactly when, but some time ago I kept recalling the masterpiece-status of *The House of the Dead*, by Dostoyevsky [Fyodor Mikhalovich Dostoyevsky, Russian novelist, 1821–1881], and I often thought of the characters in the book and laced them in our current situation. Life here is very much like the lives described in the novel, but I definitely do not mean to apply the book's title to this place. As you know, even *House*'s protagonists all hung on to their hopes; besides, not everything that happened in the book was bad. The reason I am making the comparison is that I have run across people very much like those who were so splendidly described there. While it is true that in the book we are exposed to the dark and dreadful side of human nature, it is also true that we can discover the other side there— the powerful spirit in human beings which cannot be destroyed by anything. I found that human beings in the military are much the same. Even though it will be based upon my relatively limited vision, I should like to write in some detail about a few soldiers who could not help but attract my attention. And I think that I had better restrict myself to them.

Starting December 15, I found myself in the same *han* (squad) for three months, but I was totally disappointed in the whole area of friendship. The squad members were divided between some men who on the whole carried themselves well enough, and those born militarists who on certain points are totally unreasonable. Of course I used to talk with those whom I had known since my higher school days— people like N, and another N from Waseda University, and H from the Fourth Higher School, but as it turned out I never had a real friend. I am willing to take partial responsibility for that situation, but I also think that in a very real way the military life itself was responsible too.

Every individual has, at least internally, to take a large share of the responsibility for his own life, but for those of us in the military, who are living together as Privates Second Class or Privates First Class or whatever the case may be, friendship seems to be regarded as something bothersome. I think it was mainly for this reason that I backed away from the very friendship I hungered for. I should add that two very close friends of mine from higher school days—K, who was already a Second Lieutenant, and T, who was *minarai-shikan* (a cadet) at the time—were also in the same squad. I went to see them often and they helped me out a lot, but because of the differences in rank I could not be completely comfortable even with them.

I also discovered a small but significant thing about *The House of the Dead* which I had never noticed before, i.e., that Dostoyevsky himself must never have had a single serious friendship. This is not to deny that he observed every character he came across as closely as was possible and described their personality as fully as he could—sometimes even with deep affection and a feeling of closeness. Nevertheless, and despite the fact that he spent four years in a community of exiles, the reality of his essential friendlessness strikes me as rather strange at first. Perhaps after all, this should only have been expected. How to explain the apparently unbridgeable gap which yawned between what we can see in the book about Dostoyevsky's personality and the personalities of his fellow exiles? The explanation just might be one I found for myself while trying to puzzle out my career in the military: individuals will never become really close to one another unless they are allowed some personal breathing-space. (April 24)

As part of an army division, and for *sōgō-enshū* (comprehensive training) as *kōkan* (A-class Special Cadets), we left on April 12 for Imazu Kyōteiya in Shiga Prefecture. I left with the pleasant anticipation of seeing Lake Biwa, and also of passing near Kyoto. It was so nice to ride on a train again, and for the first time in four months! Perhaps, around this time in Kyoto, you may be watching a Mieko Takamine movie or one with another such star. For some reason I was thinking of words like *shunshū* (springtime melancholy), and of yachts floating on the lake in the springtime.

> Spring is passing, birds are singing,
> and there are tears in the eyes of fish   – Bashō

I saw a fog-wrapped road sign that was made alive by Bashō's poem. I entered the Kyoto Army Hospital on the seventeenth of the month with what they thought might have been a case of diphtheria. Mr. N was there too, suffering from the same illness, but fortunately for both of us our cases were not serious. So we spent about a week just taking it easy, and looking at Mount Ei.

It was the day before we were to leave the hospital, and a spring rain was falling over my beloved old capital. In the hospital rooms soldiers in white gowns were whistling or doing things like writing postcards. Outside, cherry blossoms were softly falling past our windows one by one.

The newspaper reported the attack on Imphal. I thought of the soldiers who were killed on that occasion and that, most probably next year, we will ourselves be called upon to fight on that very same ground. We will be given the opportunity to die in this grand war of ours. Unlike some soldiers, I most certainly will not be rushing to my death; on the contrary, I want to live, and to live as full a life as is possible. I have written as I have because now I think I know enough about what real life is.

At least for the time being, I think that with this I shall have finished writing about everything that I have been meditating upon. The main point is that I am well.

It is possible that this record might become my will. Moreover, I have not written a single word about my family. Some older soldiers of the *han* have told me that you can fully appreciate our parents' *on* (their favors and our indebtedness to them) when you see them for a *menkai* (official visit). I only know that in my case, and even though I did not get to see my parents for an official visit, my love for my family is something absolute. Moreover, I find it impossible to describe my feelings and their love with my pen. "Mother" is very probably the last word that most soldiers utter, and that out of the very deepest of emotions.—Those same emotions are what prevent me from putting my feelings into words except the very word to address her.

—In the first letter from the Philippines—

Amid the festivals of my hometown,
    I wonder how my father and mother are.

—On the postcard that turned out to be the final communication—

In the March[1] skies
    the Great Dipper twinkles, and I pray

---

[1] The original phrase is "February of the lunar calender."

TAKEDA, Kiyoshi

> Born July 13, 1922. From Tokyo Higher School, entered the
> University, Faculty of Belles Lettres, Department of Japanese
> Literature, in April 1942. Entered the Navy Training Corps,
> December 1943. He was killed in action on April 14, 1945 off
> Cheju Island, Korea.

June 16, 1944   (Friday)   Clear

They tell us to "get rid of the attachment to self." But if the attachment to self is such an easy thing to get rid of, then it should already
have been taken care of long ago, say after half a year of military life.
I could not get rid of the self even if I tried. That image of myself
which I believe to be the best is something I have to cultivate, and glo-
riously, until the very end. And just how is this "self" of mine to survive—not just as a mere compromise or an outright falsehood, but in
the genuine and true sense—the vicissitudes of a military career. This
is the paramount issue for me. No one else can add anything to this or
offer me any help. And it is not something for which I would seek others' help. I must deal with this issue sincerely and intelligently, and on
my own. I am a person who could very well die tomorrow. I, the self,
am something that belongs to me, and yet not quite entirely. —Until
now, I have been pressured by my everyday life and quite defeated by
my surroundings. Moreover, I have been a vague witness to that defeat
from a spot on the sidelines, in a world so simply sentimental that it
seemed to belong to someone else. I thought of it then as a modest posture. I thought it was the heart of *shūgu*. *Shūgu no kokoro* (the heart of
an ignorant crowd)—I had made that sworn and heartfelt oath prior to
entering the military life, and over the half a year since then I had done
my best to keep the promise. I tried to achieve this by fighting down
that dear internal desire of mine to stand high in my own estimation
(and how I miss it!), a desire that urged me to throw the promise away
and wanted to laugh at it.

The heart of an ignorant crowd—to immerse myself in the masses, however, does not necessarily mean that one must destroy oneself
forever in the midst of the masses. Is now not the time to extend a hand
in order to rescue the self, the image of the "I" which somehow floated out, gasping, from the waves of foul odor? This is the image that,
amidst the ignorance and commonness of the masses, makes one
breathless; this is the self that has endured to the end after having been

cleansed of everything and having fought through every conceivable type of battle.

Taken altogether, those were days filled with considerable ennui and lazy living, but it must have been my own *Walpurgisnacht* (Walpurgis Night).[1]

Now is the time to think seriously about how one should go about living as a human being, as well as of the special problems posed by life in the sealed world of a Naval officer.

To treasure and protect the self that had survived and would survive until the end. —That I should say is the correct attitude which ought to be found acceptable even in the military life.

—Comments on my home visit—

My moods in the military life often tended to make me just stare at my feet, but the mornings that I spent at home, though only too short, furnished me with the dreams and ideals of a true Japanese.

In my home village I could both put my hand on the pulse of Japan's history and appreciate the beautiful natural features of my country. —I feel very fortunate that I am leaving for the war with all these things carved deep in my heart.

EGUCHI, Masao

Born March 25, 1921. From the Third Higher School, entered the University, Faculty of Belles Lettres, Department of European History. Entered the barracks in 1943. Killed April 16, 1945, at 9:30 a.m., as a member of Shichishō Corps, Shinpū Special Attack Forces, near Kikaiga-shima, Nansei Islands.

End of November, 1943

Greetings. Thank you so much for your kindness the other day. I am so sick and tired of the ugliness associated with always saying that "I am prepared to die" or "This is the last good-bye."

I shall not shorten my God-given natural life just out of some youthful enthusiasm. There are still so many things left which I need

---

[1] The eve of May Day on which witches are held to ride to an appropriate rendezvous. It also means an episode or a situation having the nightmarish wildness. The author is referring to the Scene 21 of the Goethe's *Faust*.

to do. I believe that, just like God's love, death will come from some-where outside (and not from myself).

On the way home, I read *Yoake-mae* (*Before a Dawn*) by Tōson Shimazaki, and I feel somewhat relieved.

We have no way of knowing whether or not those left behind (at home, not going to fight the war) are coping with the pain of having fallen in love or of concern over their children. Some others might either suffer from loneliness, or get angry about their own inadequacy, or complain about being unfortunate, or perhaps rebuke other people's ignorance. But I retain very much hope despite the whole range of these possible feelings, mostly because having them is just another proof that one is human.

War or peace—they are nothing more than a mountain or a plain in our path. So far as the traveler's fate is concerned, it does not mat-ter whether he dies in a field or on a mountain; in the mind of the trav-eler, the only thing that will last would be the very experience of trav-eling.

Now at last I am able to open my eyes wide and to see things as they are clearly. I am most grateful and owe all of this to your teach-ing and encouragement.

I will be entering Saseho Naval Base on the 10th. In the past I had considered living life to be of far greater value than making war, and had grieved over the way in which I would have to depart this life and abandon my cherished habit of reflecting on the past. Now, however, I am beginning to think that, since my idyllic existence is indeed to end, then why not end it on the battlefield?

Please say hello to everyone for me. —So long.

Masao

KURUUMI, Hiroshi

(No biographical note)

(The author wrote the following poem when he went home from the war for a break about three months before he was killed.)

—Festival of the Dōso-jin (the travelers' guardian deity)—

The red cape that I wear with my mother
as if to tease out spring in all its fullness
Snow shines with the light of a paper lantern
Falling petals of cherry blossoms touch my eye;
I am just holding onto my mother's sleeve.

The small roadside shrine was dedicated
to the Dōso-jin, where I came to visit.
I left a baked dumpling made of thread-flour
in a straw bag on the straw horse
—praying for the safety of travelers,
and packing black grains with prayers.

This road begins in some faraway place
and no one knows where it begins—
This road ends in some faraway place
so far away, but there is no real end.

Still, one continues to travel along
this road without an end.
But the traveler must press on.
My kindly mother says that
there should be some pleasure in the traveling,
and "I pray for your traveling be pleasant."

Sleeping with a straw horse
on a warm bed by the *irori* (fireplace).
Softly I dreamt of
the pleasant life of a traveling man,
moving along step by step
with a load on his horse's back.

MORIWAKI, Fumio

Born November 15, 1919. From the Sixth Higher School, entered
the University, Faculty of Belles Lettres, Department of German
Literature. Graduated in September 1943. Entered the Navy Corps
in 1944. Killed in war, August 2, 1944, just prior to landing on a
beach off southern France, en route to Germany to serve under the
Military Attaché at the Japanese Embassy in Germany.

April 12, 1943   (Takinogawa, Tokyo)

Dear Takeo and Dear Older Sister,
Dear Tamano and Shizu:

Permit me to dispense with the usual opening remarks.

I returned to Tokyo yesterday morning. I arrived in Okayama on the evening of the day before yesterday and stayed overnight in Mitsuo's boarding room. He seems to have given up all hope of recovering the (lost) trunk, but do not be overly concerned about it—and please make sure that mother is not. Mitsuo is not nearly as upset as his telegram indicated that he was.

It has been raining ever since early this morning, and I cannot go outside today; therefore, I plan to spend my time writing letters and resting, etc. It seems that there will be field training for one week (the 16th through the 22nd), and this makes me rather unhappy. I am not confident that I will be able to handle a week's training, because my physical strength is currently so low that on the way to Okayama I fainted on the train with anemia. I met Kunio of Shiokawa last night, and that helped to buck me up a little, but there are so many depressing things happening around me that there is absolutely no way of escaping them completely. Perhaps because for about ten days I was warmed up by the loving atmosphere of home, I have since become so weak-minded that ever since I returned to Tokyo I have difficulty breathing and feel about as dizzy as a deep-sea fish floating up on the surface of the water. So far as the magazine I was planning goes, during my associate's absence it was degraded to a vulgar level because of the usual politically correct *politiker* (policy). All of the best pieces, including my own, were put off until the next issue for fear of censorship difficulties. As a result, Shiokawa and I are going to leave the group. The editor's contention is that we should not risk being blacklisted by the thought-control authority from the very first issue, but, nowadays, if we have to worry so much over the matter of censorship there is no way that a fine journal can be brought to life. I feel as uncomfortable as I would be if, because my throat was choked up, I had to swallow my own vomit. Additionally, I do not know what to do with this horrible feeling of mine, one of discomfort and anger. After all, publishing is the only salvation for us at this point, and now that things have turned out as they have I regret that I did not take charge of the editing myself.

The cherry blossoms outside the window are being hammered by an icy rain. They would do better to fall instead. Yet they continue to cling onto frail calyxes while huddled up with cold and shivering. It would be sentimental to feel pity, and it is actually an ugly sight; if they fell resolutely and without much ado, I think it would be a beautiful and splendid sight. So also it is true with ourselves: The flowers that bloom late, like me, are endowed only with the beauty of falling. Perhaps one way of dealing with such a situation is to think of the icy rain as only a dream rather than as something so cold. The only possible rescue and help for a person who is thrown into a lion's cage is for him to dream a dream about being thrown into a lion's cage. Perhaps, for example, those poets who were members of the French Impressionist school were the only geniuses who could perform such miracles, but in order to accomplish such things one must necessarily have a superbly strong will. It may be that I will have to become a soldier in order to acquire such a strong will for myself. As it is, in the midst of all this psychological discomfort and contradiction, I am barely managing to survive.

Perhaps the mere passage of time will solve everything. Through the simple expedient of placing himself within the shell of thought, the dilettante or the philosopher is able to live and work without running the risk of being hurt personally. Literature, however, is the business of selling one's skin piece by piece, and so the writer must continue to fight on even with a body that is covered and cut with wounds and scars.

Occasionally I become so discouraged that it is only through writing such oracles as these that I regain my strength.

During the break, and thanks to my dear older sister's kindness, I was spoiled by her treating me to such delicious things that I developed a voracious eating habit. By contrast, it is now very difficult being here where I cannot even have a single cup of sweet coffee.

I forgot to bring the white *kasuri* summer kimono. Would you mind sending it to me at your leisure?

As for you, Mother, your work will gradually become easier. Even though there may occasionally be some unpleasantness, instead of getting angry please stay relaxed and get yourself into a frame of mind that resembles warm and genial spring weather.

Dear Shizu: Please help your older sisters in every way that you can, and be a gentle and nice child.

Well then, everyone, please stay well and cheerful, keep an upbeat tempo, and let us shake hands in parting. Sayonara.

Fumio

YAMANE, Akira

> Born November 21, 1924. From the Third Higher School, entered the University, Faculty of Belles Lettres, Department of Sociology, October 1944. Entered the barracks December 19, 1944. Died of an illness contracted on the battlefield, Changsha, Hunan Province, Central China, July 8, 1945.

—From his diary he kept during the period when he was at the Osaka Armory under the provision of the Student Mobilization Act—

June 22, 1944

The major points of my conversation with Dr. Kyo Tsuneto:........ Quite aside from the food problem, the path leading to *gakumon* (studying, searching for the truth) is strewn with thorns.

"*Trotzdem wille ich* . . . . (Nevertheless, I . . . .)"

Will May 20, 1944 be the day to be memorialized as the beginning of my new life? Just think of it—from this day on my *Wanderjahre* (wandering year) is about to begin!

> (Note by his father: As of May 20, 1944, all classes at the Third Higher School were terminated and all students were mobilized. As a result, he left home and began working at the Osaka Armory.)

For more than a week now one of my daily tasks has been to calculate when a postcard which was written on a certain day and mailed the next morning should reach its destination—i.e., me. Then I anxiously wait for that day to come, and try to anticipate what thing or other I should write back.

August 26, 1944

A human being is a weak vessel: while healthy, he works high-spiritedly because he knows that his country is counting upon him, but once his body is worn out, he wants to think only of his own comfort and to discard everything else. He anxiously starts counting with his fingers for the next holiday. Yet, he would not thrust even one more step forward to pull his feet out of the huge current of this world. Perhaps he does not have that much courage either: perhaps he has merely become a piece of machinery.

—From his memorandum book
during the period of his studies in Tokyo—

September 29, 1944.   A clear day

I was graciously told by my host that I should generally carry on and make myself as comfortable here as I would in my own home, so I spent that first night in a very leisurely fashion. Shortly after nine o'clock I went to see a friend of mine, Narabayashi, at his dormitory; after first giving me a tour of his place, we headed for the Tokyo Imperial University and he showed me around the campus. Physical conditioning began at one o'clock and was soon finished without incident. Went out to Kyobashi and paid my respects to the Imperial Palace from the *Niju-bashi* (the Double Bridge).

Compared to Kyoto, everything about Tokyo somehow gives me a feeling of desolation. There are just too few things which draw a heartfelt response from a wanderer who has come from so far away, and who was so prepared to admire. In certain ways the layout of the university itself and the gingko tree-lined walk are things like that, but I still feel disillusioned because of the great pressure they bring to bear on me. The same thing is true with the Imperial Palace—it is no more than a desolate, wild field, and the cause of any tears shed before it, in this capital city which is so lacking in charm, is something more than merely being awed.

A final thing is what I discern as the all-around foolishness of the capital's population. Does the cartoon figure Bun-chan (a little-boy), on the *koi-nobori* (carp banners) only exist in the world of *rakugo* (popular comic stories)? I think not, and if I were to speak frankly I would say that these masses of people represent nothing more than an accumulation of the trash of the provinces. When I first came to Tokyo two years ago I was shocked by the *shosen densha* (lit., wireless trains), i.e., the national railroad trains; and I was overwhelmed by the sheer crush of people. Now that I have toughened up a little; I can look more objectively on the milling throngs. —One has to look carefully in order to discover Tokyo's more positive qualities, and it would be wrong for an unsophisticated country person to think that there are wonderful things to be found all over the city.

In the evening, I paid another visit to Mr. — in Koishikawa. Ideologically speaking, I might describe him as one of Tokyo's *ronin* (masterless samurai). Although he holds liberal views, he is also very much of a stubborn, old-fashioned *oyaji* (a man of father's age), and at least he passed my own personal test for character. —Well, I shall try to be patient and to do my best, even if the dormitory seems to attach such importance to mere formality, creating a situation wherein I feel rather foolish and put off.

October 6, 1944   Rain

I went to Bunri University (currently the Kyoiku [Education] University) today. Both Professors Higo and Kato were absent, as was my friend Mr. — I returned home feeling hungry and Mr. Narabayashi invited me to join him for dinner at the Tetsudo-Hotel. It was a European-style dinner, and since I had not eaten any such dinner before I fumbled a lot, but somehow I managed to get through the meal. It was a delicious dinner of meat and fish with which I was not familiar, and I only thought about how wonderful it would have been to eat it at my leisure with chopsticks and a spoon. It was quite a job to eat with a knife and fork, trying not to fall behind the three other people who were eating in so relaxed a manner, and my efforts resulted in my being able to swallow just about half of the dinner. It was so delicious, though. The menu was soup, fish, meat, ice cream, and *Kaffee ohne Zucker* (coffee without sugar).

I have heard that a relatively small amount of rice will do to satisfy one's appetite, so at lunch I chewed each bite forty times, and was hungry again by 4 o'clock. Perhaps all this chewing so well helps the digestion too, but it is even painful to walk up steps. What is certainly no good is swallowing as I did at the dinner. You need to put some thought into how to go about eating a meal.

October 11, 1944   Cloudy

I have been suffering from a cold for two days and after my bath I felt exhausted. Since I had no one to talk to,[1] I went to bed at 9 o'clock.

---

[1]Translator's note: The meaning of the original is not clear. Therefore it is freely translated here. The word *enten* means a face or image that turns around graciously, or that is slowly dancing, or that softly and freely moves. Quoted from a Chinese classic poem by Liu Ting-Chih. Therefore, a direct translation of the original, *enten hisashiku*, would be: it has been a while since being with someone (i.e., a lady) who moves graciously.

Perhaps it is because I missed lunch that I feel so tired, and of course I realize how emotionally drained I must be. Although at this point I cannot put things as clearly as I might, I know that my current state of mind is a consequence of having tried to adjust to my new life here in Tokyo. My life is dreamlike, and I feel so helpless because I cannot get to the bottom of things no matter how sorry I feel for myself—or how much I try to fool myself.

There is one thing I know for certain: my problem is not *Heimneh* (homesickness). What it must be is my general discontent over not being able to go about living my current life in what I consider to be the best possible way. I vividly remember those days of my childhood when, though perhaps not consciously, I lived each and every day for all it was worth.

October 13, 1944   Cloudy

After classes were over, I took a walk from Umaya-bashi Bridge to Azuma-bashi Bridge in Sumida Park, following Asakusa-bashi. Asakusa is so squalid that I found it dull but, by contrast, the Sumida River in the early evening and the Kotoma Bridge are smart-looking and quite interesting. Everything was in a fog, looking as though it were an oil painting of the *Reimei-Ki* (the period of the dawning of a new age), and I recognized something very Tokyo-like about it all.

A letter came from Professor Tsunetō.

November 1, 1944   A clear, fine day

In contrast to October's rainy beginning, this is a fine first day of the month and perhaps a good omen. It is the first time in weeks that I can see clear blue skies without even a spot of cloud. It apparently showered last night, and the moist soil makes the air even more refreshing. Unfortunately, the lack of suitable footwear kept me from lunch on an excursion to Musashino. (This because if I wore a pair of *waraji* (straw sandals) they would be ruined in one day.) In the after-noon I rode the Tōhoku Line train to Ōmiya, and an air-raid siren sounded just as I was about to get off. I wondered whether I should return home or else go through with what I had originally planned.

It was a one-hour trip from where I found myself to Tokyo, and I realized that an attack on the Kanto Region meant that Tokyo had to be the eventual target. I debated with myself as to whether or not I should return to the city, even though I am not assigned to any specific air-defense unit. I had to make up my mind between the bridge and the ticket gate.

I am not one of those people for whom Tokyo is their life's blood. Since the all-clear siren would probably be sounded an hour or so after the first raid, I decided to take advantage of the interval before returning to the city. I hurried through the streets to get to the Hikawa Shrine and paid my respects there. Since it is the premier shrine of the Musashino area that surrounds Tokyo, its dignity wholly surpasses that of any of the shrines in Tokyo. Freshly repainted in Chinese red, it reminds me of the shrine of Kamo. Stifling my fear of *hajō bakugeki* (bombing attacks in waves), I moved along the eastern edge of the city. The whole area is a mixture of a diluvium plain and a lower, alluvial one, but the differences between them are at most five to ten meters in height. The alluvial land is reserved for rice paddies and most of the diluvium is used as farmland but there are still remnants of the forest. A house sits near the shade provided by the woods, and in them there are many zelkova trees and Japanese cedars. The field in front of me is a sweet potato field, and it is now being harvested; ashes will eventually be spread over that same land, and it will become a wheat field. Some sprouts are already coming up, and there are mulberry fields here and there. Cotton fields are uncommon, and those that exist only have whipped cotton. Some rice paddies have already been cut through, while others have not. Since it is a low land, there are many areas under water, and for some reason it all makes one think of June. It is exactly like the Musashino that Doppo [Kunikida, a poet and novelist, 1871–1908] wrote about. I walked through woods made up of different types of trees and which seemed to run on endlessly from the gate of an estate; here there were bamboo or cedar woods, there was a network of maples in brocade-like colors. A road crossed the path from the left, then forked off to the right; occasionally one sees stone images of Jizō (Ksitigarbha, a guardian deity of children) placed at the crossroads.

Suddenly, as I came to the end of some vegetable fields, things began to take on a neglected look, and it was then that I saw a moss-covered tomb way back in the woods. What I had first thought a private estate turned out to be a temple dedicated to the local deity. In the Kansai Region (where Kyoto is), woods are usually associated with a shrine or a temple, and not often with private homes. Such is not the case in the Kantō Region (where Tokyo is). Roughly half of the *azumaya* (a small house, a summer house) are tile-roofed, and half are not.

When you pass Chusando, i.e., along Tōhoku (the Northeastern line) —i.e., the farther and farther you get from Ōmiya and Urawa—you come upon houses scattered throughout the woods. The nearer you come to a town, the more likely the houses are to be surrounded by beautifully kept hedges, and to be topped with tile roofs.

At any rate, the all-clear was sounded after about an hour and a half, and by the time I traveled from Urawa to Tabata (in Tokyo) even the preliminary alert had been canceled.

November 3, 1944   Rain
On the auspicious day of Meiji-setsu (the day of celebrating the Emperor Meiji's birthday) we were finally hit with a torrential rain. There have been many rainy days since I entered the university but, luckily, none of them coincided with a holiday. Disappointed over having to take the trouble to eat in Hongo, I skipped one meal and then took two others, i.e., two dishes of meat and vegetables.

Having eaten, I took a casual walk around some antiquarian book stores in Kanda. I found a fine art magazine—*kostbar* (too costly), unfortunately—but could not make up my mind to purchase it. Instead, I bought a Baedeker's *Guide to Germany* published in 1913. I think this book might turn out to be historically valuable simply because all the towns which are large enough to be included in it will most probably be in ruins once the war is over.

As for meals, I have devised the following plan:

Morning (20 *sen* per meal), evening meal (50 *sen*), total of 70 *sen* a day. 21 *yen* per month (set cost); therefore 9 *yen* for lunch (per month). (Note: 100 *sen* = 1 *yen*). I set up the following simultaneous equations, with that 1 *shō* (= about 8 cups) of rice (25 meal tickets):

$$25 x + 40 y + 50 z = 9000$$
$$\left\{ \begin{array}{l} x + y + z = 30 \\ x + 2 z = 25 \end{array} \right.$$

For the solution to this equation:
x (breakfast at the university, 1 dish per day) = 21 days
y (porridge of rice and vegetables)   =   7 days
z (2 dishes per day at the university)   =   2 days

In the evening, cold evening, cold winter winds slammed against the sliding storm doors.

November 5, 1944 Cloudy. The weather improved in the afternoon. Strong wind in early evening. Quiet and tranquil at night.

I can sense that we have a full-fledged autumn already upon us. I had planned to visit the Nazu Art Museum and Professor Takagi (in the morning), and then to pay calls on Mr. Hijikata, Chie, and Ogata in the afternoon, but a single siren sounded at 10 o'clock in the morning, and caused the whole plan to fall through. About fifteen minutes after a preliminary air-raid warning siren, an air-raid emergency siren sounded; it would have been a typical siren, except for the fact that a single enemy plane had actually been sighted. The air-raid warning was cleared just before noon, but what a nuisance that one plane had proven to be! That one warning siren had served as a better alarm than ten thousand words of warning would have been to sober up the minds of those residents of Tokyo who had allowed themselves to become intoxicated by the positive aspects of the war's progress. Real tension has already been felt among Tokyoites, and after this there will be many more people who will not be able to sleep in peace. I think, however, that the enemy's intention has nothing to do with so passive a thing as a war of nerves; I feel sure that the carrying out of a gigantic air raid, and in the near future, is a major part of their plans. Given the fact that our defensive strategy is said to be in place, there should be no reason to be afraid, but how could we realistically prepare to defend ourselves (from the sort of large-scale raid which threatens)? How effective is our civil air defense? To keep our people from becoming so uneasy, we used to ask the government for appropriate instruction based on the experience of massive air-raids in other places. Of course, it would be foolish to think that an adequate defensive posture could be achieved merely by putting gaiters on legs, but perhaps something of the sort might be enough to have some effect, to cast a kind of spell which would calm people's anxiety. As an immediate measure, use a backpack as an emergency bag, and tuck in a set of underwear, heavy shirts, drawers (or long-johns), vest, woolen socks, *waraji* (Japanese-style farmer's footwear, straw sandals), towels, strings, a medicine box, and bank or postal savings-books. Even though we cannot do anything to forestall the event, it would be a forlorn fate and extremely depressing not to have the essential thing, *Essen* (food in German).

At 2:30 p.m., the preliminary warning was off. At 4 o'clock, Chie came. She brought *ohagi* (a traditional Japanese sweet-rice ball with a sweet, azuki bean covering) and *tempura* (deep fried dish). I was delighted and most appreciative, for it has been a long time since I last had sweet things to eat. —I was so thankful and so deeply touched that I literally had tears in my eyes!

I read *Cyrano de Bergerac* [Cyrano, the protagonist, was a real-life figure, a liberal ideologist of the seventeenth century] by Edmond Rostand [French playwright, 1868–1918]. The edition I read was a translation of the French play I had seen the day before yesterday. I was thinking of the time when it was written (under the same circumstances that exist here presently), and of how the season was also about the same. In the last night-scene in the park (of the Sisters of the Cross), platane (*platanus orientalis*, chestnut in the original play) leaves have fallen during the night. Thinking of the scene, I[2] picked up platane leaves from a street with a tram-car line on East First Avenue, and spread them all over; and also dropped leaves one by one from the second floor of *Shintoku-kan* (a boarding house). —(In the scene on the stage, I remember that colored lanterns in yellow and blue, etc., were used to illuminate a scene so becoming of the sad "end of Cyrano's life"! Compared to the magnificence of Germany's Tell [William Tell, the protagonist] in an earlier period, in a play by Schiller [Johann Christoph Friedrich von Schiller, German dramatist and poet, 1759–1805], *Cyrano* truly has a delicate ——— (7 letters undecipherable), an ultra-French atmosphere. Right now I am at a corner of Musashino Field, where leaves are falling from zelkova trees; while, in imagination, I am back in the time of and reading stories about Cyrano and Christian and Roxanne,—especially right after an air-raid warning. . . .

I read Yusūke Tsurumi's *Beikoku Kokumin-sei to Nichi-Bei Kankei no Shōrai (The American National Character and the Future of the Relationship Between Japan and America)*. A highly respected scholar, he brilliantly foresaw and, as early as 1922, warned about the uncertainty facing the future of the U.S.-Japan relationship. It is a fascinating book. I wonder how many Japanese today really understand

---

[2] Translators' note: The subject of this sentence was omitted in the author's writing, and it would naturally follow that the subject is the protagonist of the play; but, since there is no such scene in the original play by Edmond Rostand, it is translated here as if the author is the subject. However, the translators were puzzled by the fact that, Higashi Ichijō (East First Avenue), with a tram-car line, was in Kyoto and not in Tokyo. Yet the author was obviously in Tokyo that day, for the Nezu Art Museum and friends he planned to visit were in Tokyo, and also from other references. The author was perhaps reminiscing of another event in Kyoto when he was a student at the Third Higher School. (m.y.)

America; indeed, in my opinion we could count only a very few among us who would even *want* to understand America. And how do things stand with respect to us students? It would be very difficult to win a war without getting to know ourselves through knowledge of the enemy. Ah,—.

November 10, 1944   Cloudy
    An excursion to Musashino.
    Left at 8 o'clock. The train I jumped on at Shinjuku station turned out to be bound for Nakano (the wrong destination). Then the train I switched over to at Nakano was headed for Mitaka—wrong again! It was obvious from the start that things were not working out very well. After a while I finally arrived at Musashi-Kyō. From my past experience in the neighborhood I knew that there was no escaping the smell of Tokyo unless you walked away from the train station (of the Kanjo-sen, or the Circle Line) at a right angle and kept on walking for half an hour. So I immediately decided to walk in a generally south/southwest direction and thought that I would come upon the ruins of a Kokubunji (or, Kokubuji—an old, state-established provincial temple). Around noon, although I kept walking farther and farther there was nothing to be found but a straight street bounded by residential homes with hedges around them.
    There were more woods than I had seen in the Nerima area a day or two before, but the situation did not look good. At last, in moving from one side road to another, I found myself upon the edge of a plateau. Walking along a ridge (or, levee) which divides the rice fields, I crossed over and climbed onto another plateau on the other side (a river about two meters in width flows through this valley) which runs on for about ten meters.
    This other side of the river is mostly one huge *eulalia* (similar to white pampas grass) field, although there were some chestnut woods as well. The *eulalia* were all full of white plume, and as I kept walking I thought about how wonderful it was that such a deep field had for so long been isolated, when all of a sudden I heard *Soldarten's* (Soldiers') voices. At that precise moment I thought that I understood what it was, and I immediately turned around and backed away. Halfway down, there was a wide road headed north, and there was a half-broken fence with a sign of "No entrance allowed." I walked out from behind the fence and looked back to read another sign which said:

"Caution. Flammable. Eastern —Military Unit." I also caught sight of several *Soldaten* who were glaring at me. It was a close call!

As things turned out, it seemed that I was standing before the north gate of Tama Bochi (Tama Cemetery). I reflected on how strange it was that I had stumbled upon such an unexpected place, and decided to pay my respects at some graves. Although it is a cemetery, it looked more like a park, and this was especially true of the leaves on the shrubs which fronted the tombs; they had all turned red and yellow, and they were extremely beautiful. I did not at all experience the typical depressing feeling evoked by just about any cemetery. —Then I came upon the honor-role graves. In the southern section of the place there were the graves of three admirals: Koga, Yamamoto, and Tōjō. There was also an uncompleted tombstone for Admiral Koga. Surrounding the honor-role graves were those of Count Otoba, Shigemichi Saigō, and Korekiyo Takahashi.

After leaving the cemetery by way of its south gate, I continued westward through Tama Village, where there was an anti-aircraft gun base on the right-hand side of the road. As I kept walking towards the road which leads to Fuchu, I came upon a barbed-wire fence with a sign that stated: "Off limits to all non-military personnel, etc." I felt as though I was being chased away (as if I were being repeatedly attacked) by *Soldaten*, so I avoided them by heading north and kept on walking like mad until I finally arrived at Kokubun-ji village. I then proceeded in a westerly direction until I spotted a small temple on a hillside to the south. Although there was no name on it I knew that it must be the Kokubunji Temple, so I walked around and found Niō-mon (a Deva gate) and Yakushi-dō (Hall of Bhechadjaguru or the Physician of Souls). I walked south a little to where there was a bamboo-grass mound a meter or so above the ground around it. In the center, cherry trees were planted in a line, and at its southern tip there was one pine tree. This place is where Kondō Kōdō (Kondō Lecture Hall) used to be, and there were its foundation stones hidden among bamboo-grass—as naturally situated as they were in days of yore. There was nothing there but, at the roots of the pine tree, a single monument with a simple inscription: "An historic site: The ruins of the Musashi Kokubun-ji Temple." Leading south from this point, there was a village road about a meter wide; a long time ago this road had been used to connect the temple with the government buildings. In other words, this was all that was left of the old Sujaku Ōji (Sujaku wide road). These remains were so desolate and dilapidated that even the foundation stones could not clearly be seen beneath their bamboo-grass cover. —Were this site to be compared with the ruins of Fujiwara-Kyō (Fujiwara Capital) and Dazai-fu, I feel sure that some insight would be provided into the Kantō Region people's cultural impulses.

There are so many woods in this area composed almost entirely of chestnut trees, and all of them as cultivated as fruit-tree gardens. Some among them, of course, are intentionally left to look as though they are natural woods, and in these places the autumn grasses are truly beautiful. Among other growths there are railroad chrysanthemums, thistles, bluish purple bell-shaped flowers—that I do not know the name of—and tiny red pepper-like things.

These chestnut woods surround the usual woods of zelkova trees, chinquapin, and other trees that are common around estates. Fronting them stand some slightly yellowed mulberry trees, and there is a cultivated field beyond. The mulberry occupies about a quarter of even the cultivated field, so as a result the whole scene has a yellow base. The entire wood—with its layers of dark green, or the reddish color of its zelkova and cherry trees, and yellowish green mulberry trees—is absolutely beautiful. The fields are mostly sweet potato fields which, once the season is over, will become wheat fields. There are some *daikon* (Japanese radish) fields mixed in with them, and a few persimmon fields as well. About half of the fields in the Nerima area are reserved for cultivating such vegetables as the Japanese radish (some cabbage, too), but around here far fewer are used for that purpose. There are no woods around Nerima except for those which belong to estates, and in the suburb of Urawa such woods surrounding estates deepen and begin to look more like natural woods that are composed of different types of trees.

I have already mentioned the plenitude of cultivated chestnut woods around here, which explains why such plants as tea and cedar are planted as hedges. I did see something similar to this arrangement in the Nerima area—a field surrounded by a variety of short shrubs— but there it is used more to mark property and is freely accessible. Things are stricter here; enclosures cannot be entered and private roads come with gates to keep people out.

Around Urawa even these sorts of hedges do not exist. When you see a sign asking *kaidashi-butai* (groups/troops of people from the city who come to the countryside to buy food) to stay off the property, it is not difficult to imagine how popular this area is becoming. Many factories are being built, and there are clear indications that what was once purely a farming community is undergoing a transition. My impression is that this is the most beautiful of the three (places which I have visited and written about), but my general analysis of its current prospects is not very positive.

MATSUOKA, Kinpei

Born August 10, 1923. From Shizuoka Higher School, entered the University, Faculty of Economics, October 1943. Drafted and entered the barracks, December 1943. Killed in action in Moulmein, Myanmar (Burma), May 27, 1945.

Diary

September 27, 1943

What is Fascism, I mean really? Is it a reactionary movement in opposition to that era which, beginning with the Renaissance, seemed to signal the triumph of rationality and science? Are authority, pure experience, instinct, and the power of creative imagination, as Morris Cohen [an American philosopher, 1880–1947] wrote in *Reason and Nature*,[1] all phenomena that were brought about by anti-rationalism? As I see it, the definition can be given in one brief line: Fascism is the escapism of our time. As a consequence of that dead end of the awakened consciousness which followed the Renaissance, I suppose that Fascism is something that was pushed forward in an attempt to make some sort of a logical advance. To deal with this contemporary society of ours, which has reached the ultimate in confusion, the easiest way would be to make an appeal to divine inspiration. As a rational society becomes more and more complex, it is only natural for its government to take pains to build unity. However, a solution to a given society's state of confusion, a confusion which stemmed from that same society's rationality, needs to be looked for in a strictly rational direction. Alfred Rosenberg [in 1930 he expounded a race-theory in his *The Myth of the Twentieth Century*; lived 1893–1946], a pet of the Nazi leaders, stated that, in Nazism, Germany had found an ideal political form for the twentieth century. A Nazi nation was created by arousing the masses through the creation of a temporary emotional high, and

---

[1] Cohen, Morris R., *Reason and Nature: An Essay on the Meaning of Scientific Method.* 1931.

then dragging them around in total blindness. . . . But an emotional high is just a temporary thing, and what would the blinded ones find themselves in the middle of when they are once awakened from it? All sorts of liberty is stolen away via government control, and the only thing left would be the government itself—a government that demands complete submission from its people. A very powerful constitutional state would indeed remain, but that same nation would soon fall victim to a logical contradiction. Under the pressure of any rational criticism it would be forced to face the reality that its self-destruction is imminent. —So do not allow yourselves to be drowned in Fascism. Fascism is a temporary excitement which the young are likely to get into. We should be cool and calm and straighten up the disorganized situation: we should not leave behind a source of trouble for a hundred years to come. Right now, Japan is caught up in this sort of excitement. To be so excited would be all right for the masses, but those who are to be bulwarks of the nation should never allow themselves to be distracted by harsh and temporary emotion. Be calm, take up the sword of rationality, and untie the confusion.

Finally, I too have to move off to the battlefield. The privilege of academic deferment[2] has been abolished, and the time for us students to help fight the war has actually arrived. I cannot explain my feelings right now except that everything seems so complex and weird. After working hard and getting through the national educational system, which is known as the Ginza-dori (i.e., the equivalent of New York's Fifth Avenue or Park Avenue) of learning, and even succeeding at entering this Tokyo Imperial University, I have at last been able to reach this point. I, who in three years (or, rather, in two-and-a-half years) would be in a position to take my place in society as a full-fledged scholar, am now leaving the university and departing for the front because of the nation's demand.

Am I unwilling to give up my life? Perhaps that may be the case. For a human person, it does not even matter whether we are speaking of totalitarianism, or of the relationship between the whole and indi-

---

[2] Temporary exemption from conscription: The government measure offered temporary exemptions from army service to young men who were either enrolled in school or were living overseas. Certain limits to the extension of these exemptions were set by revision of the Military Service Law after 1939. Step by step, the exemption was lowered from the original twenty-seven years of age to twenty-six, and then to twenty-five.

viduals, or of any such thing—as if we understood them in the first place. —In the final analysis, the one clear-cut point of view is that, when all is said and done, what one has left is oneself. To push my logic a bit more, I would have to think that there is no such thing as a completely selfless person in the whole world. Any person who thinks in terms of the nation and of the whole picture is one who is trying to see beyond that point where the whole and the individual are in harmony, that is, they are the people who were in search of locating the point where the whole and the individual connect. A soldier is supposed to show selfless devotion to his country, but can they all say for certain that they have given up self? Soldiers may be seen as noble just because their occupation—what they are moving toward and directly facing—is war and death, and in the nation's defense.

An idea that death possesses an infinite value lurks in everyone's mind, but, in the final analysis, is this anything less than a descent into materialism? I am talking to those of you who consider that merchants who sell an item and make a profit are simply materialistic, and that those who set their hearts on money-making are despicable and their thinking simply filthy. What it all boils down to is that, according to this philosophy, absolutely everything, death included, can be converted into "matter."

At the same time, we have to be made aware that there is absolutely nothing, regardless of how minute it may be, which has no soul or spirit. Since human beings are what they are by their very nature, I should think that not one of them is totally bad clear through. Even in the case of a thief who is about to steal money from someone else, if you investigated not only the thief's direct or immediate motive but dug deeper in search of an explanation for his thieving, I don't think that what you would come up with would have much to do with evil for the sake of evil. Once one takes such things as his family situation or environment into account, some good would be found even in a thief's heart. Once you follow this line of thought, then, it generates a caste of mind which contends that any phenomenon, no matter how small and insignificant, is all spirit. —Death is certainly at the top of the totem pole, a fact made most clear in the phenomenon of taking one's own life—which is the crowning-point proudly played by the heart which is facing "matter/thing" squarely.

I do not understand it. It is a fact that I cannot find an answer to this whole question of "matter/thing" regardless how hard I have tried.

. . . . The *Daikyoku* (what is believed to be the origin of everything) definitely exists. I can "believe in" the existence of a god or gods who ultimately control the world of human beings, and indeed the whole natural world. Someone has said that belief is power; *true* belief certainly has infinite power, as well as the key to the final solution. Are we then—or rather, am I—capable of unquestioned belief? Perhaps it is due to my ordinary and shallow character, as well as to the impure heart which will always form part of it, that I cannot believe what is offered me to believe. There, *jashin* (a sinister heart) always enters. It is truly regrettable.

I have learned about the *teigen meirei* (categorical imperative) that Kant talked of, but what it all amounts to in the real world I cannot say. What I get out of it all in the end is something like a theory on the emotions. And the fact that I am writing as I am now may be ascribed to nothing more than a temporary high (the excitement of a moment). Perhaps in the future some time may come when we can laugh at all this and put it down to the psychology of youth—either something that might be expected of any man who went through the higher school education, or it may merely be a form of dialectical thinking. To speak more plainly, it may all end up as pointless arguments for argument's sake, which strikes me as very sad. —When I am writing, or doing something that I passionately believe in, that is my truth. That emotion which enables me to act even though I may be laughed at as just an idle dreamer for doing so is stronger than any other. Ah, but what on earth is the reality? What would be the limits to a human being's ability to control his thoughts? What are human beings supposed to do? What am I supposed to think? What could be proven to be the solution to it all? I was distracted as I was writing, so let me get back to my original argument. Even though I realize that it is not everything, I certainly do not wish to give up my life. My seniors, and now I myself and even those younger than I, are all dying off as they get into action. Death. Death. —What is death, really?

I shall leave that question unanswered. Older soldiers, and my own generation as well, are all getting killed or injured in the effort to build-up Greater Asia[3] and to ensure our own nation's peace and tranquility. Let us leave aside those who are merely injured and think of those who are being killed. They are dying, hoping for and believing in the con-

---

[3] An expression that was used to justify the war of aggression, pushing the idea that, with Japan in the lead, all Asian nations would prosper.

struction of Greater Asia and the maintenance of a prosperous Japan. The same is also true with me. Those who are killed can rest in peace if and when the establishment of Greater Asia and Japan's prosperity have been achieved. But what happens if those goals are not achieved? —In the latter case, the dead will have to carry the burden of their regrets beyond the grave. Someone has said that a war is easy when you are winning, but becomes very difficult once it turns into a defensive struggle.

Speaking out straightforwardly, I should ask the government whether or not this war, in which Japan is now engaged, is being fought with any probability of winning? Cannot it be that the government is forever fighting on with only an empty dream of victory? Can they tell us citizens with any degree of certainty that Japan will definitely win? Are there not always some nearly impossible conditions attached to any such positive assertion? Oh! But my argument eventually comes to founder on the rocks. Only the students majoring in natural science are allowed to stay on at universities, and the rest of us have to move on to the battlefield. I can no longer find a solution for this uncomfortable feeling I have about my personal predicament of having to face death. I am almost about to fall into an anti-war ideology; perhaps I already have. It just might be that, once I enter the barracks, there will be an end to it. Then, perhaps, I shall not think about anything, and it is possible that would be the happiest path of all; for the more I think, the more contradictions I find myself involved in. Man, however, must be a "roseau pensant." (from *L'homme n'est qu'un roseau faible, . . . mais c'est un roseau pensant.*) i.e., a thinking apparatus. Even though human beings do have the ability to think, they do not possess the ability to solve all problems. In the final analysis, human beings are also meek and lack courage, but to have no ability at all must mean that there has been no effort. I certainly studied so hard, and made my very best effort to try and solve anything and everything; but it was just a one-scene dream. It was a dream of a dream. Mr. Kiso told me of his reaction to having completed the physical examination for conscription. Placed as he had been among the ordinary people, he told us how intellectually superior he had felt and made us feel the same way. He said that the written tests could easily be finished in a minute or two. Perhaps that may be true. I know from personal experience that I completed the written exam portion of the archery-ranking test in about one-fifth of the time it took other people to do it. I know it is true that situations of this sort exist. Yet the more one looks at those above, one becomes aware that (the knowledge) is so vast. So it is that I have to study very hard for the examinations at the school, and put all my effort into preparing for the university's entrance exam—even though I find books on economics as tasteless as biting into sand, and become sleepy whenever I begin to read a law book. One consolation is that the academic world is still very vast. There is still no limit to the number of unknowns, even though world-class researches have been carried out. Indeed, *gakumon* (i.e., intellectual pursuits and learning) is forever. In the opinions of those of us who are searching for eternal truth, there is nothing more meaningful or worthwhile for a man to do. Compared to this search, something like a war is no more than merely a one-scene comedy. I would think that, facing absolute truth, military expansion might perhaps be seen as less important than the making of a spider's web. —Human beings are weak, however, and for this minute phenomenon (i.e., war), I have to sacrifice my researches into eternity.

What today's human being is hoping for the most is "peace." What does the word really mean? If we were into a discussion of true peace, we would have to realize that such a thing will never come until mankind is no more—there will always be other wars over such things as natural resources, the state of the economy, etc., even when the military conflict is over. The subject of the morality of war has occasionally been discussed in recent books, but can there be such a thing as the morality of war? Anyone who kills a man will most certainly be sentenced to capital punishment, simply because he killed a man. It is obvious that people are killed in any war, so how can we morally accept it? Does this mean we have adopted a morality that accepts people being killed? There is repeated emphasis on the broader view, on the general good. But if we are to look at a war from a broader view and with the general good in mind, why can they not set things up in such a way that it is not necessary to kill anyone? And how, even while killing people, could they possibly make a distinction between a broader view in favor of the general welfare and a narrower view? All killing is evil. To give life to a dead person—any such proposition is nothing more than an example of the contemporary philosophy's kissing up to an unpleasant reality. Philosophy should be something that leads people. To attribute either life or morality to those who are gone would be an insult to our civilization itself, as well as a man's self-deception concerning his own actions.

I saw a movie, *Muhō-matsu no Isshō* (*The Life of Lawless Matsu*) [a movie directed by Hiroshi Inagaki, played by the famed Tsumasaburō Bandō and Keiko Sonoi, who was killed later by the atomic bomb]. Perhaps due to the state of mind I was in just before entering the barracks, the film left a particularly strong impression on me. I was able to enjoy it as one of the best shows in recent years, and seeing it will remain in my mind as a most memorable event. ....

Memories of things in my past such as field days at school, lantern marches, the sound of (festival) drums, etc., all run through my mind as though it were a revolving lantern itself. Everything has disappeared into the past as if it was all a faint dream. I wonder when I will ever get to see a lantern march again, and when I ever will be able to soak myself in the pleasure of a field day. I am about to lose my mind! I want to beat a drum. I want to be part of a lantern march. And I yearn to see the long-sleeved kimono.[4] War, war, war: this is all much too strongly a fatal matter for me right now. This world is absolutely dark. What morality can be found in any war? A war for fulfilling one's greater duty? What is one's greater duty anyway? —All that is nothing but a fool's sleep-talk. So long as I feel that it is to be my fate, I would not give even the slightest thought to having to go to the battlefield. However, is this really the answer to the question of my fate, and will this world ever be able to return to peace once again?

Let them call it liberalism, militarism, or totalitarianism: they are all means to an end. Japan must walk, and is walking, her own road alone. If the war's goal had not been the achievement of peace, then what else could it have been?

Perhaps it is uncertain whether or not the years around the 5th year of Shōwa (1930) and after was a period of true liberalism, but I know what Japan was like then and I miss those years. I miss the past. I want to keep on chasing the dreams of the past.

I do not know how to cope with today's reality, and feeble-heartedly pursue faint dreams of the past. I dream a shallow dream of victory in the future—like a castle in the air.

Be far more strong. —I want to become much stronger. That's all.

---

4 Translator's note: the fancy type of kimono worn only by a young maiden at very special occasions.

ARISAKA, Nagao

Born February 2, 1918. Entered the University, Faculty of Belles Letters, Department of Japanese Literature, from the Tokyo Higher School. Entered the barracks March 1942. Killed in action in Assam State, India, April 1944.

(Letter to his younger brother, 1)

I feel very good about the great fraternal efforts we are putting forth at this splendid moment in history.

Perhaps you remember that when I was a university student I always thought of how important it was, in addition to being a student, also to achieve a self-awakening which was deeply rooted in history. One must always be determined to attain such a self-awakening.

Words can be made to say anything, but there is no way for anyone or anything to come alive except when they may be thought of as part of one's own problem.

We who have experienced our own particular personal histories would naturally attract people's notice and draw society's attention, so please think seriously about that while you are still in school. After all, we have more responsibility than we may realize; so never lose confidence and never forget to cultivate magnanimous feelings.

(From a letter to his younger brother, 2)

Up until about ten days ago I kept carrying the letters I received from you when I was still in central China. On nights when the full moon shone brightly I used to walk about the barracks' perimeter in a state of high excitement as I reread those letters of yours.

With regard to your state of mind, I tried to learn as much as possible by using some imagination in reading through your correspondence. At the time I was convinced that a human being had to learn to think on two levels. It may be a bit confusing, but this is only because it reveals my method of explaining original propositions by first carefully verifying the facts behind them and then tracing them back to the original.

Bunretsu (a splitting, dissolution) simply means that a person does not have to remain his same, simple self forever. Most probably, the absorption of any really deep truth requires the possession of something like inner eyes. One must continually be re-forging the self—

over and over again, and must cut through the membranes that entangle themselves around that same self.

In order to keep attaining an ever higher degree of *tōitsu* (unification) a thorough training of one's inner eyes is imperative. For this to come about, it will not do to be overly impressed or emotionally moved by just any object you may run across. This amounts to nothing more than merely encircling the object; if you really want to get a solid hold on something substantive, the best approach is to encounter the object directly.

Of course someone who is twenty years of age is entitled to insist on the rights of twenty-year-olds: my only hope is that, even if you do not follow my path of literary study, you would suppress rootless emotional behavior in favor of grasping something substantive. But that is enough writing for one day. If you have found anything unpleasant about this letter (i.e., if I have in any way offended you), please forgive me by attributing it to my *katte* (taking liberty of . . . , or, self-centered carelessness). —Please respect your own convictions, and I hope that you will mind your health.

SAKAMAKI, Yutaka

> Born June 17, 1921. Through the Urawa Higher School entered the University, Faculty of Belles Lettres, Department of Education, in October of 1942. Entered the barracks December 1 1943. Died March 11, 1944 in South Korea of an illness contracted while in service.

(A letter to a lady with whom the author had been a friend for some fifteen years.)

November 17, 1943
My dear Miss Oda:

It has been almost a month since I last wrote you. My favorite stationery is all gone now, used up with the last sheet that I sent to a close friend. So many things in the past come to mind even when I am writing as casually as I am now. This may be the very last letter I shall be writing as a student, and I wonder whether or not I shall be able to write to you again. At any rate, I am moved to consider the uncertainty of a life that is here today and may not be tomorrow. I would like to beg your pardon and ask you please to read a bit of this letter even though it is badly organized. I simply needed to write to you, even though it is only about a part of my feelings.

As always, I will begin by updating my current situation. So far as the wood carving goes, although I tried different ways and worked hard, it did not live up to what I had in mind. So I finally gave it up. I plan to begin again fresh at some later date, once I am fully in the mood.

I do not know whether or not you feel the same way, but I think that people nowadays are losing religion, and that we cannot really connect with any of the established religions. Given the miracles and its theory of *kyūsai* (salvation), I cannot fully accept Christianity either. So too with Buddhism; as for Shinto, I feel like asking whether or not it is something we ought to believe in. It seems to me that we have actually lost the object of our faith, especially in Japan: when we look back upon our past history, is it possible to find any "being" that we should believe in?

Why have I begun to write about faith all of a sudden? I should state it plainly: it is because in the near future I shall be facing certain death. Human beings have always had religions because, from birth, we confront the inevitability of death. The religious sentiment begins with the realization of how powerless and alone one is. From that point, one goes on to hope for the existence of someone who does not stand as an equal to the self but is somehow absolute. Mankind calls this absolute being "god" and, by single-mindedly placing the self in a humble position before him and pouring out our heart and mind to him, believes that the individual can escape the world's calamities. Faith of this type, however, is a product of only the most primitive religious feelings, and at the present time is the type of faith or religion which it would be impossible for us to have.

When I said earlier that we *have* lost faith it was this "faith of the heart" that I was referring to. Perhaps we could call this "faith of the heart" a *soboku* (simplistic or unsophisticated) faith. Ever since the time of *Man'yō-shū* (lit. *Collection of Ten Thousand Leaves*, the oldest existing collection of Japanese poetry, in twenty volumes) we Japanese have lived considering *soboku* to be the most fundamental *seikatsu kanjō* (emotion or feeling about life). Recently I wanted to bring my own emotions and feelings about life to some sort of conclusion, and so I searched for a key among the Japanese of the past. Ever since *Nihon-gi, Nihon Shoki* (*Chronicle of Japan*, the oldest official history of Japan, completed in 720) and *Man'yō-shū*, Japanese feelings of this type have been primarily and most thoroughly expressed through the term "*makoto*" (sincerity, true heart, honesty, fidelity, etc.). Onitsura caught the meaning of the term when he described "*makoto*" as a natural emotion expressed in a natural way, i.e., after the ancient fashion of the simple (unsophisticated, or even naive) Japanese expressing their own feelings in an entirely natural way.

"*Makoto*" also refers to the statement of true facts in true words. The ancient Japanese who truly lived lives of "*makoto*" were both morally good and logically correct; and they were also people who lived aesthetically through the internal and simultaneous expression of those qualities. It was in this way that they were able to express themselves so sincerely in such poems as:

> If I went (to fight) on the sea, I should become
>> a corpse soaked in water, and
> If I went (to fight) in the field, I should become
>> a corpse from which mosses grow
>>> —in any case, I shall die near the emperor, and
>>>> Without any regrets.

Or:
> Beginning today, I shall not look back, since
> I am leaving (for battle) as a humble shield for the Emperor.

In this spirit they were able to fight the emperor's war with clear and pure hearts. As I face the fact that combat is fast approaching, I ask myself whether or not *I* could lay claim to such a pure and simple heart.

Both of the two poems above emphasized the notion of "not looking back." But then what exactly does "not looking back" mean? Concretely speaking, we might perhaps think that it means father and mother, brothers and sisters, wife and children, personal wealth or fortune, honors, power, and so on, but I would think that the most direct reference must be to life itself. The issue of life and death is something that every single human being must forever agonize over and try to find answers to. Moreover, this is not something for a publicly appointed genius to find an answer to, but is rather a subjective problem which every individual has to face. I think that in the cases of those unsophisticated people—the ancient Japanese—they were as one in their ability to transcend this life by means of their simple faith in following the emperor alone.

Those who can rely on such a simple faith are fortunate indeed. The modern mentality has forced us, and to an excessive degree, to become aware of the individual's own mind, and now we are no longer able to disregard the self. We have resolutely managed to mold a complete microcosm within ourselves, and we even seek *kami* (the absolute person) within us. We are the sum total of our existence, and so what our death amounts to is in fact the destruction of the cosmos of ourselves, i.e., we can only be what we really are while we are still alive. I should say that the most agonizing time of all has come for those of us who have lost the simple faith of our fathers.

We are heading for the battlefield, and although of course war does not kill every single soldier, it is quite certain both that a great many will die and that we each have to be prepared to be one of those casualties. In other words, it is no overstatement to say that we are now facing death head on, i.e., that whether we like it or not, we are forced to come to immediate terms with this issue of life and death.

At the time when the student mobilization plan was published on September 22nd, we university students were terribly shaken and three of us kept talking on the subject with great emotion until very late on the evening of the 23rd. Beginning on the evening of the 30th, we continued the discussion until 4 a.m. Additionally, even daily correspondence and discussions were not quite enough to contain our urge to monitor that situation. All this amounted to, however, was a temporary excitement, and there were as yet no realistic feelings about what it would be like to be conscripted—let alone any feeling of urgency about death. Soon that initial excitement dissipated, and what constitutes a problem for us now is just one thing: the necessity of facing death on the battle-field. We are not afraid of death itself, but we are agonizing over how we can resign ourselves to giving up the life that is the best and the most beautiful possible.

I am sure you must have heard before that in Japan discussions about the problem of life are always based on pretty much the same approach, and especially when the discussants are those who are called thinkers or advocates—or even so-called philosophers. They are certainly different from those Western ideologies which, ever since the atomism of Leibniz, have been based on the philosophy of the individual. Japanese ideology seeks the attainment of eternal life through a simple and complete union with the emperor. That is why it is said that by dying for the nation, a Japanese can live for all eternity. Let me pick up a copy of *Shisō* (*Ideology*, a monthly journal) by way of example. In the November issue there is an essay by Junji Takashima entitled "*Taisen-ka Gakusei no Mondai*" ("The Issue of the University Students during the Great War"). —Let us simultaneously read and critique the essay.

> "In the mind of the individual citizen in our imperial nation, what to sacrifice oneself amounts to is the just attainment of eternal life.... However, while its exact meaning is the determination to undergo immediate physical death, this decision to sacrifice oneself for the nation also involves the *kakugo* (psychological readiness) for *gyokusai* (a death of honor). . . . Both the decision in favor of a death for honor's sake and making oneself psychologically ready for it are unrivaled and most noble accomplishments. They are also very difficult things which require a foundation of unshakable belief. One's belief is strengthened by one's earnest though sorrowful wish, just as the wish is itself strengthened through resignation. Resigning oneself to this particular reality is something that requires immense courage. . . . Reflecting upon one's own life, and facing unavoidable death . . . in order to meet death head on, a person must transcend it and live his life as truly as possible. To live a life truly a person has to grasp the fact that his own life is *jikaku-teki sonzai* (a self-conscious existence) and that the only way to elevate it to its highest possible value comes through joining it with the one who already possesses that value—i.e., to devote and sacrifice it to the sacred person."

What the essayist is trying to say is something which I can sympathize in general, and his way of saying it, is obviously not just an instance of publishing something for publication's sake. What it all amounts to, however, is nothing more than stating something that is really self-evident in a formally structured way. Even with regard to its substance, there is nothing to *shisa* (suggest/indicate) that there is anything special about it. For example, I myself have already discussed in a general sort of way this whole business about a man giving up his life for the nation. This is a purely conceptual notion, totally *anjin* (Buddhist terminology: to ease one's heart), and it should be considered as an entirely different issue—quite separate from life as it is really lived. The author then went on to indicate that the expression "physical death" might be discussed in terms of the following diagram:

Momentary life			Eternal life
Physical life	⇨	Physical death ⇦	Lacking life
Practical life			Ideological (abstract) life

Additionally, the author himself recognizes the difficulty of establishing physical death as a realistic problem, but he fails to offer any substantive explanation of how either "*shinnen* (belief/conviction)" or "*higan* (pathetic wish)" might overcome that difficulty. His other position, i.e., that "a resigned view of reality" can be achieved through the exercise of "extraordinarily great courage," is also nothing short of an insult to those of us who are serious students of philosophy. The new problem or question for all of us who are searching for ultimate good and ultimate beauty in our lives and who have a deep attachment to life would be the simultaneous possibility of "commitment to a physical death" and "resignation to reality."

I would think that to "reflect upon one's own life and stare at inevitable death, *and* to meet death while doing so" is certainly the truly idealized *mononofu* (warrior's) mind set, but just how can overcoming death be "living life truly" at the same time? Then again, when the author makes the obvious reference to the emperor as "the only sacred person," one might ask just what way of thinking about life would make perfect union with him possible.

Here we see the hollowness of the author's whole argument, by means of which he is attempting to affirm realistic, physical death by arguing that it will evolve into eternal life. In other words, he is attempting to transform "inevitable death" into "a positively meaningful death," and that is where I see both the weakness of his argument and a jump in logic. When one grasps his life as a conscious existence, and by way of following one's own will he "elevates it to something of the highest value"—that raises the question of what is the highest value for all those of us who live a conscious existence. The author's discussion is vague, and neither should we engage in casual discussions about it.

At any rate, the author argues that ". . . understanding reality by means of self-reflection is the source of true strength. There is no one as weak and as dangerous as the one who, by deliberately clouding his/her sagacity, neglects to look straight at reality and prefers blind reliance on their own strength. . . . It is only through the deepest concentration that winning through in the end would be possible." In this way he makes a strong argument for the necessity of having a solid world view—and this is something that certainly *is* necessary.

Perhaps this discussion of life-and-death issues has gone on long enough, and in any case I have arrived at the following conclusion:

> It is just and right for us to live our lives through to the end. To be right and just is natural for us as human beings, and is a state most suited to the gentle and true/sincere heart. However, we, as members of a larger, collective entity, must respond to the needs/requests of that entity. Our response(s) may mean death, but this is where "the resignation to see reality clearly" comes into play. The problem, however, is that reality reaches its height at precisely that point where it is most difficult to see clearly. I would think that in order to overcome this difficulty one would have to go beyond the "seeing" stage and enter the world of "action"; no, one must rather reach a still higher level and enter the world of *kangyō ichijo* (the union of observation and action) that the Buddhists talk about. If that is the state of mind which we cannot experience and recognize in a relatively short space of time, then does that mean that we can never escape being a prisoner of carnal desires?

KOMORI, Juichi

Born December 29, 1922. From the First Higher School, entered the University, Faculty of Jurisprudence, October 1943. Entered the Navy, December 1943. Killed in action, January 22, 1945, in the Philippines.

July 5, 1944

To my dear friend:

I wonder where I should begin to write to you. Perhaps this is because it has been so long since I last wrote my usual lengthy letter describing my innermost feelings. Lately I cannot think of those fancy words that I used to write with many decorative phrases, and with the exciting development of ideology that made my heart quicken; they do not come to my mind, either. So, this note may be something that will bore you. If you should get bored, it is all right if you light up a cigarette, or even interrupt with a casual conversation, but please do me a favor and read (this letter completely) as an old friend.

At any rate, what am I to write about? As I am thinking about it, a dim evening of quiet rain seems to draw me into thinking of the past. Somehow I cannot help missing the past so dearly. When I close my eyes, this image and that smile come up. In my desk drawer, I found that snapshot that you gave me. I wrote on the back of it, as you know, the first poem of the very beginning of *Faust*:

> Ihr bringt mit euch die Bilder froher Tage,
> Und manche liebe Schatten steigen auf;
> Gleich einer alten, halbverklungnen Sage
> Kommt erste Lieb' und Freundschaft mit herauf;

> (English translation:)[1]
> You conjure up delightful days and places,
> And there ascends so many a cherished shade;
> Like an old legend's half-forgotten graces,
> First love's and friendship's echoes are replayed;

But, as I was looking at the snap-shot, I thought, as Faust did, ending—:

> Ein Schauer fafst mich, Träne folgt den Tränen,
> Das strenge Herz, es fühlt sich mild und weich;
> Was ich besitze, seh' ich wie im Weiten,
> Und was verschwand, wird mir zu Wirklichkeiten.

---

[1] *Faust*. Translated by Walter Arandt, New York: W. W. Norton, 1976, p.1.

(English translation)
A shudder grips me, tear on tear is burning,
With softening balm the somber heart they have;
What I possess I see as from a distance,
And what has passed, to me becomes existence. . . .

I am writing this in that kind of state of mind. That is to say, I am placing myself back to a half year ago, and talking to you of my half year of life in the Navy, as a reminiscence of long ago. Therefore, I am afraid this will probably become something vague and intangible. Actually I feel as if I am dreaming a dream, and also outside it is cloudy with the moon shaded by a long continued rain—that is the situation.

This was during the Navy Training Corps period—the period that is not totally lacking in nostalgia when I look back, but at the same time was the most upsetting time in my life. When I entered the Naval Training Corps which was frozen with cold military rules and strict confinement, coming from the Higher School where we so fully enjoyed applauding the freedom and thinking of liberty, how desperately I desired for love. Even the powerful urge of my pure heart worrying about the nation was suppressed by the upbringing that never permitted even a slightest deviation: so I simply wanted love, i.e., so-called "detestable sympathy" that Nietzsche [Friedrich Wilhelm Nietzsche, 1844–1900] spoke of.

There was a man named K in my unit: K had a frail body and delicate sensitivity, and, was, at the same time, also a poet who wrote about his tormented emotions. When he stood with me for night watch in the cold evening of December 31, he rumbled a *tanka* poem:

> In the cold evening of December 31,
> I am going to sleep without a lyric

It was indeed a cold night. It was the night I helplessly watched K, who was physically not strong, lose an oar off a cutter in the sea, and be beaten up by the head of the teaching unit; I think I wrote you a letter that evening, too. In the postcard, I think I wrote a not-so-well-written *haiku* poem:

> In the evening I am writing
> To a friend who is ill, it is freezing cold

but is my memory wrong? That night, even more than the black earth outside, my heart, and even more so K's heart, were freezing through and through. The joyful day for me, and for K as well, to leave the Naval Training Corps approached. For K, who was in the third year of the Tokyo Imperial University, needed to have the confidence to pass the qualifying exam to be a *shukei minarai I-kan* (probation intendant officer of I-rank, i.e., midshipman). Some bright hope began to color his poems.

> Father and mother must be awake
> As I look at the skies over them, my heart is filled—

One day he confided in me a certain concern. He said that he was arrested while he was at a higher school, and was kept in jail over a half year, for "a thought problem" (i.e., leftist ideologies), although he ended up judged not guilty and there was no indictment. What happened apparently was only that, in a cultural magazine, for which he was one of the editorial committee members, a *senpai* (someone senior to him) contributed a leftist essay. Also, in fact, he has the light heart that is natural to a poet, and he has nothing to do with something like a leftist ideology which is so uptight and dialectic. Most certainly I brushed off that concern of his lightly, and K seemed to be completely relieved, I thought; but, yet, I had a slight concern over him.

About what happened after the announcement of the result of the exam, I assume that you can imagine from his poem:

> Calling my father and mother, I am under the deep winter snow,
> I am totally helpless

and also two of mine,

> Under the depth of winter snow, I am there silently
> Not knowing what to say to a friend so despondent

> While I thought I might look as if chiding a despairing friend
> I was talking to him that he must have a brave heart

It may be true that he has a black mark in the past, and also that he did not possess the personality most suited for a soldier, but his soul was so pure, without any stain, almost as if it is heaven itself. You would understand how tough and painful the life of a sailor is, particularly for a man like K. At any rate, in the night before we were to leave the Corps, he attempted to commit suicide, and I found him and stopped him from completing it: the fact is that I was troubled and felt pain in my heart for a long time, for I was not sure whether that was good for him or not. I guess I wrote much too long about K, I am afraid. But this fact made a very strong impression upon me of how harsh this world of human beings is. I leave you to be the judge.

Tsuchiura—the cradle of our *Umiwashi* ("Sea Eagle" i.e., Navy Flyers), where the morning sun reflects upon the clear water of Kasumi-ga-ura Bay, and the setting sun casts red over the Tsukuba mountains—is where I faced death for the first time. As you know, before I entered the Navy, I wanted to solve the issue of life and death by relying on the teachings of either Christianity or Buddhism. And by following Bankei's teaching of so-called *Fushō*[2] and also accepting the Zen phrase by Taikei, "*nōteki-teki chi, nichi-nichi kore kōjitsu*" (roughly translated, "Each day is a fine day as the bad and the ugly fall to the earth, drop by drop.") I felt I was reasonably able to gain peace of mind. However, it was nothing more than a view of life, with living as the base, and death as *Nirvana* (or more literally, the other shore). In other words, viewing death, separate from the physical being in the abstract sense, was like lining up life and death on the same rank.

I heard that young pilots and others in the battle field say that, when going to fight one battle after another, and when physical pains increase to the highest point, death becomes so irresistibly attractive that they volunteer themselves to go to the place of death. When all the theoretical frills are removed, my so-called *anshin ritsumei* (spiritual peace and enlightenment, or calm resignation to fate) philosophy must also have been in fact something not profound as in the above situation.

Was it last spring when I saw at the Teikoku Gekijō (Theater) the scene of *Faust* in which, using a curse, he called upon the *chirei* (the spirit of the earth). Yet, because of its excessively horrible and severe appearance, he covers his face?

---

[2] The Buddhist monk, Bankei (1622–1693), was critical of the formatized Kōan Zen Buddhism and advocated Fushō-Zen. He contended that every person is born naturally with "the merciful heart of Buddha," and the goodness in people is *fushō fumetsu* (i.e., it has no beginning and is indestructible), not something that is acquired, and is eternal.

One day a single plane belonging to the Kasumigaura Air Corps made an emergency landing, and fire erupted. The door to the *fūbō* (windscreen) could not be opened, and all on board were tragically killed in front of our eyes. We, who could not do anything to save them but could only watch, could see clearly how they thrashed about with pain and died, and I think I could even hear their screaming voices.

To me, the face of death was just like that of the spirit of the earth in *Faust*. Since this one glance at that, I was forced to reexamine my view on life and death.

Honestly speaking, to begin with, death became far more frightful and something to hate, than I thought before. Serving the fatherland necessarily has to depend on such a cursed death like this? The problem inevitably is naturally shifted to a consideration of the fundamental ideology about the condition of the correlative existence between the individual and the nation. In other words, as I faced harsh and actual death I was pressed to reexamine and reflect upon what I used to talk about—death as "the beauty of giving up the self" by viewing death rather romantically. My diaries of those days bluntly show that.

However, as you know, I am an optimist, and also quite lazy. Without being able to find a solution for that question yet, I came to this unit.

And the war condition is increasingly tense as the enemy is approaching Saipan; so, a kind of *takkan* (farsighted view)—perhaps I should call it a sense of resignation—was born inside my heart, although I cannot quite call it a solution. The fact is, at the present time, I should say that people like you may be much more exposed to the peril of life than I. Up until now I think I had held a certain contradictory ideology—what did we call it in philosophy?—that a self-sacrifice with all one's might for the fatherland will inevitably bring about death.

I remember the time when you and I talked about God (or gods) on the dormitory's rooftop, as we watched the faraway clusters of stars, several hundred light-years away. "The 'clear intent' that wraps around the Milky Way" or "divine intelligence" or whatever you may call it: "something that is absolute" is not necessarily something that is hard and dry, I would think. While being swept away by fortune, yet I am attempting to test that fortune: is this my human arrogance?

My beloved fatherland's beautiful mountains and rivers, the people who love me and warm my heart—in order to protect all of them, I shall muster all of my strength. And, if I could have a pleasant way of sacrificing the self, as before, I shall follow that path. Even if the death that is to be hated and cursed should be there, I guess that cannot be helped. If I could have a one-in-a-million chance of the good fortune to survive, there will be an opportunity to visit with you, laugh, and drink together. My thinking now is something like that.

It is ten minutes before the lights must be turned off, and time is up. I am afraid that I have just kept writing things in a rambling manner. It is still continuing to rain so faintly outside. The skies under the second-guard-disposition are dark, but (would you believe that) my heart these days is quite bright.

> There are the days, wind shines, clouds shine,
> And new trees also shine

I will be writing you again. I pray for your good health and studying.

YAMANAKA, Tadanobu

> Born March 5, 1922. From the Third Higher School, entered the University, Faculty of Belles Lettres, Department of Ethics, April 1942. Entered the (Naval Training) Corps in Kure, December 1943. On August 15, 1944, died at Yokohama Naval Hospital of an illness contracted while in the Navy.

(A portion of the diary which he kept while at the Otake Naval Training Corps.)
December 31, 1943

Even in a place that is far removed from the *shaba* (the non-military world), the holiday time brings that certain special joy which is typical of a New Year. Even for one who is as close to this joy as tomorrow, I somehow feel a sort of pity for humanity in general. No matter what, this New Year's Day falls right in the middle of my fifty days at the Naval Training Corps, and it is time to make a breathing space. At any rate, the New Year is a joyful time as always—regardless. Perhaps my life may be a very long one, but at this particular point in time I must not think along those lines.

I need to separate out the next one, two, and three years, and the time leading up to them, as a distinct unit in my life. Proceeding under this assumption, I must, in a way, put a sort of conclusion to my youth.

I cannot believe that what is going on in my life is real, but indeed it is reality. I thoroughly dislike the military, but I have to stop thinking this way. Is this history or what? It is certainly a mystery that makes no sense to me.

Human beings have a name for this: they call it history. There is something totally mysterious behind the things that happen, the things that come out of nowhere. Individuality is being blindly destroyed as we find ourselves in the middle of a world which we can make no sense of. Totally strait-jacketed and pathetic as we are, we human beings who live such lives are richly deserving of whatever sympathy we can get. Lately, and despite myself, I cannot help but be easily moved to tears. So frequently have I become homesick, and thought of so many things—how much I wished that I could have lived a better life, been more composed, more open-hearted; how much nicer I could have been when I lived at home, and so on. More than twenty days remain during which I shall have to go on with this kind of life, and I truly hate it. I wish that I could get out from under this predicament even a day early, the sooner the better. The military makes a human being into a nothing. It seems like a place where you would train animals in order to make them tougher.

(Part of the diary he kept while he was at the Takeyama Naval Training Corps, a branch of the Yokosuka Naval Training Corps.)
March 10, 1944

I must adapt myself to my present life, and then resolve to live though it with an attitude of resignation. It would be of absolutely no use either to struggle or to despair. Must I then become a blind man and a fool? No, not at all; I do not have to be either. What I do have to do is continue to survive in this situation as long as I can and remain a human being in the process. I must make a pretense of blind obedience in order to deal with the unsatisfactory circumstances in which I find myself. So far as *geistig* is concerned my entire mental and spiritual makeup is completely opposite of that of the military man. I am standing at a window in these rundown barracks of ours staring out blankly at a scene that is made hazy by the spring rain. —I wonder whether or not the scene bears some relation to human nature itself, and perhaps to society at large as well.

Integrity of life—this is both an *Ideal* and a *Beginn* (a beginning).

By contrast, the hard reality is only this indecisive life which is somewhere between being depressing and being lively. My life situation is such that I do not know what the future may hold, and as a result I feel very miserable and helpless. I look forward to my leave—but for what? I spend a whole week just looking forward to a leave, which is nothing but sad commentary on the dreariness of my current existence. What a worthless and meaningless thing it is to reflect on the fact that the road I am traveling is short and that at its end is death! Shall I end my life working so hard just to fulfill the most basic of human desires?

June 22, 1944

After I leave here, I have to go through about four months of technological training, and be commissioned, then I will be sent to the front line, either to deal with more of life—or death. I am psychologically prepared for whatever I have to face, but I do not wish to think much about death. It will simply come when it is time for it to come. There is nothing for me to do but to follow the dictates of my fate. And I do not wish to make a big thing about arranging for a will, or other such things. The only treasure I am leaving behind when I die will be my *Tagebuch* (a diary in German). Until the time comes, i.e., in the limited time I may still be allotted to live, my only hopes are that my own life might be fulfilled and that I can very carefully protect this *Tagebuch*. A record of a truly and a seriously lived life—is it not enough to have this? There is no need to be impetuous: one should calmly wait for one's time to come. I am inclined to feel like being alone. At the times when I am experiencing high personal feelings, I am reading *Begiff der Angst* [by the Danish Existentialist philosopher Sören Aabye Kierkegaard]. There is no high and no low in my *Tagebuch*; neither is there any superiority or inferiority. There, only the total self exists, and if I simply manage to express myself in it, that is enough.

(Part of the diary he kept while he was at the Fujisawa Electrical Surveying School)
August 1, 1944

Lately, I have somehow regained enough composure to be able to think. These days, I finish each day's work in a very bureaucratic fashion and then, in a manner of speaking, I keep looking at myself. I am not stepping—not even one step—outside of my personal affairs. Quietly, without a word, I am protecting myself. It may be *egoistisch* (egoistic) but this is the only way it can be. I truly feel that I can identify what is meant by *"Denker"* (thinker in German) with my own experience. The *Kōryō Jihō* (the Third Higher School's journal), which I borrowed from my friend Nakamura, is a very pleasant reading experience, particularly for nowadays. I have read through *sumi kara sumi made* (a corner to a corner, i.e., every word in it) repeatedly, and have been very favorably impressed. I was touched very close to the heart by an essay on Valery, by one on subjective morality, an original work by a young author, and so on. I felt how powerful the Third Higher School must be in order to produce such vital people even in such times as our own. I wonder how they managed it.

If someone, via telescope, were watching this world from the world of stars, he would be witnessing a masterpiece of drama in the process of unfolding. Even I have a *rolle* (role), perhaps a bit larger than a thousandth of this huge drama of history in the making.

I am not the type of person who can just stand around and watch as a bystander—I have to be right in the middle of things. How is it going to be? The wheel of fate has begun to turn, and it does not know when to stop. I hear that, within this year, we will have the end of the war in sight. I wonder what sort of an end it will be? At any rate, we are being toughened up for the confrontation. Further, the process follows a single, specific form; and in it the self is vanishing more and more into nothingness.

I have a sort of pitiful feeling. I feel as though I, the self, am vanishing away totally into the movement of history, a movement which is surpassingly vast and immeasurable.

YAMAGISHI, Hisao

Born October 29, 1913. Through Shizuoka Higher School he entered the University, Faculty of Engineering, Department of Architecture, April 1937, and graduated in March 1940. Conscripted and entered the barracks, January 10, 1942. Sent to battlefields in Manchuria and the Philippines. Died from a combat-related illness, July 28, 1946, at the Tokyo Ōkura Hospital.

—In Northern Manchuria—

The horsetails I picked make me feel nostalgic,
  for it was at just about the same season when
    my sister used to pick them at home.

—White waves (En route to Manila)—

I wonder whether or not my family members know
  that I am out in the midst of the ocean's waves,
    And advancing to the south.

A string of my thoughts is now disturbed
  since I must take my departure
    without having received any letters.

A red roof is visible on the shore.
  I am going to let my wife know that
    I am arriving safely at Manila.

—Cebu Island—

The shadow of the moon in Cebu is hiding
  behind the leaves of trees where the evening breeze is blowing
    with the fragrance of sweet papaya.

—Homesickness/Nostalgia—

I shall never forget the springtime
  in my hometown where
    a bamboo-grass stream and green fields are so beautiful.

(Translators' note: These poems are written in a
Japanese verse-form, the *tanka*—5-7-5 7-7 syllables.)

MORIMOTO, Hirofumi

Born March 8, 1923. From the Eighth Higher School, he entered
the University, Faculty of Jurisprudence, October 1942. Entered
the Navy Corps on December 10, 1943. Killed in action on
October 14, 1944 in the Taiwan area.

(A letter to his father, February 11, 1944)

Dear Father:

Today is *Kigen-setsu* (February 11, Anniversary of the Emperor Jinmu's accession).[1] The skies are so clear but the wind is very strong. It is that famous "*kara-kaze* (a dry wind) of Tokyo" that blows very strongly around February and March. Even when I was staying at the Mori's home and returned from the University on days when the skies were clear, the surfaces of the *tatami* mats were sandy. This place where I am currently is especially dusty because it is reclaimed land and the sand and dust are horrendous; when I returned from the athletic field, where the ceremony of reading an Imperial Rescript was held, my fancy officer's uniform was white (i.e., covered with white sand). Right now I am looking outside and not doing anything in particular. The ocean is glittering, but for some reason I am feeling rather sad. My barracks unit is built facing south, and when I think that my older brother is at the farthest end of that direction my heart is sucked into the horizon of cloud or fog and I feel as though I were dreaming. When I was at school I did not write to my older brother at all because I was so selfish, but since I joined the military I have come to realize so clearly, and for the first time, how terribly I miss home and how much I long for letters from home.

Even though we are members of the military, and those of us here are right in the middle of the capitol city of Tokyo, I still am feeling melancholy. My older brother is doing his best in a faraway foreign land, how much he must be thinking of home, and how anxiously he must be waiting for a letter from home! If it were myself, I think I would most certainly go crazy. Please write to him, even if you have to skip a letter to me in order to do so. It would be great if each of you —Father, Mother, older sister, Kazuo, and Yachiyo (his younger sister) —would hand-write to him individually. With our *magokoro* (sincere and true heart) we have to protect my older brother who is so important to all of us. Regardless of whatever else happens, we cannot allow him to be killed. I am reminiscing about the time when I played the *Shōgi* (chess) game with him at the entrance way of the living room with the warm spring sunshine playing over us. I am anxiously waiting for those kinds of days to return to us. Dear Kazuo, make sure that you enjoy the wonderful comfort of being at home. At the present time,

---

[1] One of the four major holidays in Japan at that time. It is the *Kenkoku Kinen no Hi* (National Foundation Day) today.

however, I am afraid that, no matter what I say, you would probably not fully understand how great it is to be home.

(A letter to his father, February 25, 1944)
Dear Father:

I received a letter from Mother yesterday evening. Yours came even earlier, on the 15th, and I am sorry for having shown myself to be so discourteous by failing to acknowledge its receipt. The fact is that I was as downhearted as, more recently, I have been benumbed because of the unusual cold of the last two or three days (the day before yesterday was especially severe, and snow accumulated even as much as three inches yesterday morning). I was depressed because, while I received a letter from the Mori family on or around the 13th, there had as yet been no letter from home. Apparently (your letter) got mixed up and mistakenly ended up with the *minarai s shikan* (officer cadet class) just ahead of us (which includes Mr. Sahara). I am so very happy that those letters were brought to me yesterday. In addition to Mother's letter, I also heard from Yachiyo and Aunt Yamashita, and yesterday had a whole parcel of letters from the sports teams of the Eighth Higher School. Moreover, the skies are very clear today and it is much warmer, perhaps because the snow has all fallen. It would be great if, riding on this trend, springtime comes early.

Mother's letter touched me to the point of tears. I am especially delighted since I read about how pleased she is with my becoming an officer cadet. I shall continue to study even harder, and I will conduct myself in such a way as not to let down my homeland and everyone back home, and not to fall short of my fortune's (goddess of fortune's) expectations. I am grateful to you for having shown respect and gratitude to the *ujigami* (a tutelary deity, a *genius loci*) and also to the Shiojiri Temple. The god(s) my mother believes in are indeed miraculous in their efficacy. One has only to look at my older brother for clear proof of this. For him to come out of so fierce a battle as Guadalcanal alive was due to two things: first to his physical and mental strength, and especially for the magnanimity of his character when dealing with subordinates, and the other is the power of our Mother's faith in the *genius loci* and *fudō-sama* (Scala) of Narita to say thanks, and if there is time I will certainly go along with her.

That reminds me of a surprise visit Mother paid me at my boarding house last April. Because a telegram was delayed, I was completely surprised when I returned from the University and Mrs. Mori said:

"Your mother is here." "Can it really be true?" I responded, hurriedly taking the stairs two at a time and immediately opening the sliding door. I will remember how choked up with tears I became when I saw Mother's peaceful, sleeping face.

This was at a time when I was in the worst possible shape and had nearly suffered a nervous breakdown. I could not even feel either the beauty of the cherry blossoms in Ueno in Tokyo or the energy of the young leaves shooting out of the gingko trees. Worst of all, and no matter what I saw or heard, I could not cry. But I remember that at the time when I saw Mother's sleeping face, and only then, my heart was choked up somehow and tears filled my eyes. I also deeply regret that at that same time I treated Mother as carelessly as I did. I suppose that I was behaving as strangely and obstinately as is perhaps typical of someone who is so weak-hearted and is in the habit of keeping his own emotions secret. I also deliberately used some such expressions as "Narita-san Corporation" in order to offend Mother.

Still, I would be pleased were you able to believe that I hated those priests of Narita who were taking advantage of a woman who truly believes in Narita-san. I am sure that, at least to a certain extent, this was in fact the case. At present, I truly regret that, at the time, I neglected other ways of expressing my thoughts, and I should never have said a lot of the things that I did say. Indeed, from around the time when I was in my third year at the Eighth Higher School and my first year at the University, I was fretting and generally behaving like a spoiled child. Even when I came home from school and we were together face to face, I often made out as though neither of us wanted to be with each other, and would return to Tokyo without ever having said anything at all that would please your heart—you who had waited so anxiously for me.

After every such occasion, however, I was struck by a terribly powerful loneliness, and wondered why I said this and that and acted in such a manner. Even as the train was rocking me along, such thoughts made me very deeply contrite. (Often on such occasions, Father and Mother, I could not help but imagine that you had both been taken from me.) —Dear Father and Mother, please let us take care of ourselves and live long lives.

YAMASUMI, Kan

Born March 12, 1923. From Hiroshima Higher School, he entered
the University, Faculty of Belles Lettres, Department of Japanese
Literature. Entered barracks December 1943. Killed in action 6
p.m. August 12, 1945, near Mi-hsien Chitang village, Honan
Province in Northern China.

—For Professor Ōyama—

One planting of white, another one of red flowers,
    I planted *sasanqua* plants as a keepsake.

Some asked if it was not an unlucky plant?
    But I chose *sasanqua* plants
        because I myself am confronting death.

—To Mr. Shunsuke Kimura—

The summit of Mount Fuji must be covered with snow;
    I keep thinking of it these evenings.

—A poem left at home—

Winds are howling and the night grows old.
    I am rubbing down a black ink stick,
        As I wait for tomorrow and departure for the war.

—Birds—

A flock of birds are flying past each other
    In the direction of a deserted and dilapidated house
        whose surrounding wall is broken and the dirt crumbling
        down.

Several hundred crows, some baby crows among them,
    are cawing and flying over a ridge line.

—A Quail—

As I walk on a grassy place where tiny flowers bloom,
    A bird suddenly explodes right at the bottom of my feet
      with a loud flapping noise.

—Wild Geese—

Since everyone says that wild geese are on the move,
    I looked up and saw them migrating through the clouded skies.

In the gathering dusk the skies are clouded over
    and wild geese are floating away to the west.

The field of Manchu is now in late autumn;
    the grass is withered, and the wild geese
      seem to be heading south.

(A letter to his father around the time the author graduated from *Yobi-Shikangakkō* [Reserved Officers' Cadet School])
My Dear Father:

I have finally found an opportunity to write you, so I am taking advantage of it.

Since my assignment to China, my company commander and others have made a request to our superiors (on my behalf) about some vacation time for me, but that request was rejected. I understand that, by rule of law, once we join a company on the continent (i.e., China), at least two years must pass before one can again step onto the soil of Japan. The *ku-tai-chō* (the district commander) has also been very kind and sympathetic, and he told me that he too was not permitted to go home from the time when he graduated from the Preparatory Division of the Military Academy until he finally left the battlefield as a lieutenant.

Perhaps one might call it merely *guntai-boke* (a military daze), but now that there is no longer the joy of looking forward to graduation day, I have fallen into the habit, upon awakening in the morning, of staying in bed without moving for as long as an hour and a half. When I think of how disappointed you must be, Father and Mother, I also think of all the *fukō* (acts contrary to filial piety) that I have committed up to now.

If it is possible to say that there is such a thing as a positive element in all this, it is that, anticipating that what in fact has happened just might occur, I brought along with me at least the bare minimum of basic books. —Also, I am sending photographs to you by this messenger. They were in an album, but I took them out because the album would be too bulky. I may ask that it be sent to you from Hsiping or somewhere. If it is, please place the photos in it following the numbers. This week is so busy because of the preparation for graduation: there are still some days, but I am going to begin by making a list of things that have to be done.

It would be one thing were I to be stationed in Peking or some other place where transport is available, but otherwise please send me some books now and then. *Bunko-bon* (pocket-book editions) of Wilhelm Meister or some collection of poems would be good examples of what to send. —After I read them I will probably be forced to leave them behind, even though I know there will be some I should keep and carry with me wherever I go—while others, of course, I will not.

Since I entered the military I have come to realize deeply how wonderful were the circumstances of my earlier life, and especially how wonderful friends are. I am very grateful for my friends of the past, all those crazy guys. Of course even here I do have someone to whom I can open my heart, but most of my current colleagues are different from the old ones.

There was a lecture by the *seito-taichō* (student commander of the unit) yesterday. It began as a stiff (frowning) lecture, but very quickly ended up as random chatting once alcohol began to take its effect. In the evening I had dined at *kutai* (section-unit) with others. My companions were very nice, and poured *sake* for me; I think I drank at least about 3 *gō* (about 20 oz.). It was a splendid dinner, and at the graduation ceremony we will have another dinner sponsored by our three *chōkan* (superiors).

There are so many things that I would like to talk about, such as the memories of field training, the Manchurian people, the cold, about Hsinking and the school, and so on, but I think it is time to stop writing.

Father, I think that by this time you must be well past fifty years of age. In this place I even forget my own age, and I am such an undutiful son that I cannot remember even my own parents' age unless I concentrate.

The war has reached a critical stage and the battlefield may soon encompass the Japanese mainland itself. Please take good care of yourselves.

(From his last letter)
> I have become quite accustomed to sleeping in a Chinese house,
>> But the dreams I dream every night are about my Father and Mother.

> In my dream my mother has tears in her eyes,
>> but in reality she has great strength
>> —So please do not cry, my dear Mother.

SHINOZUKA, Tatsunori

> Born January 27, 1923. A graduate of the First Higher School, he entered the University, Faculty of Belles Lettres, Department of Education, in October 1943. Entered the barracks, December 1 1943. Died of an illness contracted on the battlefield, January 31, 1945, in Santiago, Isabella State, Luzon Island in the Philippines.

Children's songs are among my favorite things. I like folk songs too. According to Mr. Kunio Yanagida, folk songs are the natural products of the hard lives led by people in a certain area. Folk songs come out of the mouths of local people in order to bring some comfort into their difficult lives. They are always composed of the same sentiments and they are handed down from one generation to the next. Some of the very oldest folk songs are said still to carry traces of the Nara Period. It seems only natural then that the study of folk songs would glimpse into the nation's primitive past. It also seems likely that there is something about them which appeals to Japanese hearts and sentiments in a special way, just as it is probable that those which lacked this appeal were somehow forgotten and disappeared. The same is true of children's songs and especially of nursery lullabies, i.e., that the words and phrases included in them also change as time and generations pass. These changes are traceable to the fact that phrases which made particularly strong impressions were sometimes moved into other contexts.

Sleep, sleep. Where did the nursemaid go?
She went over the mountain, and into a town.
What gifts is she going to bring back?
A chest of drawers, a *nagamochi* (a large oblong chest for
    clothing),
    and *hasamibako* (a *daimyō* box; a lacquered traveling
    box carried at the end of a pole).
If your expectations are that high
Don't let them think of dismissing her.

It was raining, but we still went out for field training again today. When I ran with my weapon, and then flattened myself on the ground, there were lovely dewdrops on the soiled grass leaves. It was a quiet world there, so totally different from the one in which I am training for war. It is said that "*seijaku* (quietness)" gives birth to greatness; there was certainly a tiny and beautiful world hiding there. "There is a large world in a tiny thing if one keeps looking at it." These are Tolstoy's words, but, indeed, there is a hidden and elemental mystery in these truly lovely dewdrops. A heart that can dare to "look intensely" at a tiny thing—something like that is what we need at present.

There was autumn dew on the *hagi* (Japanese bush clover;
    Lespedeza bicolor) blooming in the autumn field,
    —and swaying in the autumn wind.

MISAKI, Kuninosuke

Born March 8, 1921. Through the Tokyo Higher School, he
entered the University, Faculty of Belles Lettres, Japanese
Literature Department, April 1940, and graduated in October
1942. Conscripted in July 1944. He died in an infirmary north of
Taisher in Siberia (as he was taken and detained by the Soviet
Union after the end of World War II), April 10, 1946.

(Letters to Mr. H)

Sorry about not having written you for so long. How are you? I am well too and am working in good health. Each day I can clearly see how the winter is deepening, and I am amazed by the evidence of the forces of nature which are headed toward us. Even when I stand on the very same patch of ground I stood on a day earlier, and look around, it is almost shocking how much the winter has done in just one night. The feeling of the flaky red-brownish pebbles which crunch under my boots—whether you wish to call them rocks or just hard chunks of soil—is surely different, and colder, compared to yesterday. It is something like the feeling one gets, back home in Japan, when the soles of the feet come into contact with hard, frozen little columns of frost.

Hereabouts, there is nothing in sight that we would call a tree, but even those things which might be said to remotely resemble trees have lost all their leaves and stand there in semi-nakedness with no flair. The same is true with a small shrub that is shorter than a man's height. There are no real shrubs here, i.e., none that compare with those commonly found in Japan, such as azaleas. Here, in the middle of a place where everything green has disappeared, one only catches sight of two or three branches growing from a thin stem so pitifully.

I thought, how will these sad-looking things manage to grow sprouts when spring comes round again? But when I took a close look at them I saw some buds; moreover, only the branches with buds grow out into the shape of arches that are tilted towards the sun, much like fishing rods that are at once supple and tight. Perhaps they are silently showing their desire to be as near the sun as is possible. Compared to the leaves, all dried up and dangling downward in brown shade, those branches, even without a single leaf, that are tenaciously standing up toward the skies with at least some life in them, appear so much more strong and reassuring. I reflect that our present situation should also be more like those branches. —I thought too that those leaves, dead and yet hanging on, were like dead souls.

I trust that you are well as always. I am all right and more or less just passing time. The last time I wrote something about tree branches and such, but since then, through observation, I have learned a lot more about these sorts of things. For example, in my book on German copper-plate prints there is a painting of Mary holding Christ and sitting in a fenced-in courtyard near a single dead tree. I have forgotten the artist's name, whose work somewhat predated Dürer [Albercht Dürer, 1471–1528], but his is truly fine art. I liked the print very much and, no pun intended, even feel that it left its own imprint on my eyes. Its powerful effect is especially enhanced by the fact that, aside from the mother and child, the only thing inside the enclosure is a single dead tree. When I took a closer look at a pitiful dead tree which I encountered in this neighborhood, it seemed to me that it and that tree in the painting were one.

I think that now I can clearly understand why that artist painted the dead tree. He painted it not only to remove certain elements which might, from a copper-plating perspective, prove problematic, but to symbolize the human condition wherein one's heart is purified of everything this-worldly, and finally stretches straight heavenwards with resilience and even a sort of ripeness (pointing towards the possibility of that other-worldly life which is the highest and the only true product of life in this world). I am ashamed of my own ignorance in not being able to see such a simple thing until I had examined that pitiful dead tree in the middle of nothing but unruly grass. At the same time, I felt and still feel such respectful awe over the artist's eye and technique, both enabling him to transform nature into art so vividly and splendidly. On your next visit to my home I would like you to take another look at that *gashū* (book of paintings/prints). I would also like you to ascertain whether or not I am correct in remembering that dead tree has an arch-branch which points to the sky. I have written to you just because having made such a small discovery has made me so very happy. Please laugh with me!

I have not written you for a while on the assumption that you continue to do well. I too am trying to get as much as possible out of every day. When I wake up in the morning I find that the windows have frozen over, and they look like a piece of frosted glass with one huge design. The sun first strikes at the very top of the window and you cannot see anything outside.

The snow is no longer melting, not at all. The skies are clear and the sun shines continually, but it brings no warmth whatsoever. All that the sun can manage to do is to bring out a chilly but striking contrast between the pure white color which covers the ground (and all man-made items as well, including all the rather pedestrian square buildings) and the clear cobalt color of the horizon which separates them so clearly. For some reason I do not much care for a sun that, instead of shading warmth, only brings about beautiful color combinations, and it all serves to strengthen my certainty that the dead tree I have been speaking of is not meaningless. Moreover, that is not the only thing: the fir trees with their luxuriant foliage which is so pleasant to gaze upon—the *nire* (elm) trees, the zelkova trees, the *yamake*-zelkova trees, the *nara* (Japanese oak), and the *hinoki* (Japanese cypress), the *kashiwa* (evergreen oak trees)—and so on, are no less spiritual than a pitiful dead tree. Fine as that painting is, I should think that it would be more natural if it included sunlight that was warm, abundant, and "productive." At last I begin to understand why Goethe, who had such a totally flexible and well balanced heart, felt the way he did about the Roman classics, and why he was eager to admit that the "sunny Italy" which he so admired made him more productive.

If I had to be stuck in some poor and downtrodden section where only a poor dead tree could be born, I should hope to survive and even to learn something from the experience. However, and if it were at all possible, I would prefer to be in a Faustian situation, living pleasantly on cleared land (and with *frei* [free] people, too), where, if a man worked hard and kept his confidence, he could beat back the waves of infertility and see to it that nature became productive. *Mikawa no tami* (the citizens in Mikawa) of Asahi Kaikan have as yet not quite risen to that level, but they show promise and possess a certain charm. —I need to study a lot more.

Sorry for not having written you sooner, but I trust that you are well. As usual, I too have been going about my everyday business, but here lately I have been thinking along the following lines.

With respect to artists: (I know I don't have to be so formal like this, but) it would be all right for an artist who is truly worthy of the name to be a bit clumsy, and not one of those people who can do whatever needs to be done at any one particular time. But this clumsiness of his—and especially in matters pertaining to the running of his own life—is probably unavoidable and should be accepted as a matter of course. He probably feels more powerful than ordinary people do about pursuing the right course of action, and the breadth of his response to all sorts of human emotions is probably wider than the rest of the population's. But if the artist is in his own way a sort of possessed human being, it is important that he should express that energy of his only through an objective piece of art rather than overtly and in raw form. His emotions must be purified by passing them through the work of art. It is precisely because he is so possessed by what you might call *sōzō-teki shōdō* (the creative impulse) that his actions are not in conformity with those of our own. This same possession explains why he is so ragged about running his life, and the truth is that he is close to being in an out-of-control situation.

Neither does it matter whether or not the artist's work corresponds with the taste of less gifted people, or with their shallower emotions either of joy or anger. The reason for this is that when the artist's work is unfinished but still in its natural state of development, then and only then can what the artist considers secondary events in the world at large become purified and incorporated into a form that will prove well nigh indestructible—and every event is transformed into a real part of the finished product. Whether that product will be useful or not is not the point; in reality, it has only become such as it is by way of each stroke of the artist's chisel and/or his brush.

The same process is not limited to the genesis of a monumental work of art. Whatsoever work it might be, it is more than a matter of having had to finish by a specific time registered in hours and minutes. Anyone and everyone who has ever created something new—whether he or she be a farmer, fisherman, driver, carpenter, stonemason, politician, doctor, grade-school teacher, or soldier—they are all true artists in the history and the development of that work. In his theorizing on landscape painting, Rilke made a distinction between philosophers and artists, but, instead, I should prefer to say that, were he a true scholar, a philosopher would be an artist as well.

Again I have to apologize for not having written over such a long stretch. I am truly embarrassed by my laziness in responding to your kind and frequent letters. Well, it is spring now, and I am feeling so much about so many things that I will not bother putting them in any particular order. I am sure, Professor, that you remember the beautiful painting of Sandro Botticelli's in which he depicted Venus appearing on a scallop in the middle of the waves of the Aegean Sea, and that you also recall that strange-faced god of the western wind standing near Venus. Halfwit that I was, I passed over its much deeper meaning and simply thought it was a beautiful painting. —Anyway, the days here are beginning to feel more like spring, and day after day a steady western wind is lifting up the sand dust. A western wind is what brings the springtime, and such beautiful things as flowers and green leaves with it. As to why Botticelli painted the goddess of beauty and the god of the west wind so splendidly, I cannot help but think that he too must once have been in a place where a strong but lukewarm western wind blew over him every day. Indeed, this *had* to have been the case.

It is no coincidence that when in his advanced age Botticelli became a Christian who attributed everything to the Lord God of Jehovah alone, he could no longer paint. After all, in the context of Greek polytheism the Lord God could not come anywhere near Venus. In the painting, some beautiful flower petals like cherry blossoms are scattered around Venus's beautiful curly hair. I can imagine Botticelli painting the picture while he was smothered in the beautiful scent of flowers carried by a western wind, and by all that it implied. —Once denied that pleasure, I suppose that he could no longer paint.

When I followed an old woman on her way to sell green onions and walked into an old town, I smelled something which I thought very strange even though I did not know what it was. In such places, there are still many middle-aged or older women whose feet are bound, or who wear a gold ring through an ear. The gold rings are not bad at all, and the little ones even look nice. In general, however, the binding of feet is a very distasteful thing. When these women walk in tiny steps, I wonder what is good about the whole process. Of course huge feet are unsightly too, but I find those small, triangular, and unnatural feet simply repulsive.

I understand that *Erziehung* (upbringing, breeding, education) involves some pulling or drawing out by *Ziehen* (twinge, ache), but even if beauty can only be obtained through some sort of *Erziehung*, even then I absolutely believe that this cannot possibly be brought about by such a process as binding feet. There is a book by Schiller entitled *Ästhetisch Erziehung*. This book could certainly not be understood by those who believe that an unnatural and tightly binding process is the only mode of education, or who think something like bound feet beautiful. We are, however, surrounded by so many officers who give such instructions.

It really gives me an odd feeling to note that, while people have an infinite variety of faces and bodies, yet the tips of those women's feet are all the same. If people exist in an infinite variety, as they do, it would only be right for each person to differ from others from the tops of their heads to the tips of their toes—it is a good thing for each person to be physically arranged in an individual way. So, this strange custom of totally ignoring each person's unique individual personality by making toes all the same is indeed disgusting. At least young women nowadays are not following the custom, but it makes me sick to reflect on the fact that, considering our current mental and emotional makeup, there may be many things which resemble that procedure.

When spring arrives at last on a western wind, the beautiful thing is the color of the soil's surface. The orderly ridges of fields are truly beautiful too: not yet tilled or even green, but they remind us that people have worked on them until last autumn. Such orderly lines are delightful to eyes that have only been accustomed to looking at vast, dry stretches of dead fields. Field fires burn almost every night throughout the surrounding mountains, and, at their fiercest, we could see a thin red line spreading out here and there, even in the daylight. When we look up at them in the evening, they do not have the horror of homes on fire, but rather they look really gentle (though I am certain that if you went near it, it would be seem to be burning intensely enough). They give me the same feeling as those red charcoal fires that have burnt themselves out and become dead silent. Once I happened across such a burnt field and there was nothing left but scorched, dead weeds—nothing interesting. But when multitudes of dandelions and other flowers suddenly shoot out all over the charred black mountain surfaces and surround us, and when new, fresh green sprouts begin to come out, everything turns green within three days. This eye-opening change of colors, from black to green, is something that I could never have experienced back home in Japan. There is only one thing that I do not yet understand, (even though it is often discussed,) and that is the emotion with which people in this snow country greet the arrival of spring. My puzzlement stems from a conviction that it would be more accurate to consider this a land where there are only winters and summers. At about the same time the mountain surface turns green and is clouded over by warm rain; the river flows so abundantly, and the tilling of fields begins on a huge bar in the middle of the river. Ferry boats also begin to pick up their activities. Along the river, I can see a Korean woman beating her laundry with a stick and rinsing it with the river water. —The first vegetables to appear are green onions, striped with contrasting white and green layers that penetrate our eyes. Elderly women put them in baskets and go into town to sell them, and I have never experienced a pleasure that rivals that of the fresh and harsh smell of those green onions.

(A letter to Mr. Rokurō Hidaka)

Sorry I have not written you for so long. There are no changes here. Is everything all right in Kamakura? Since there is no talk about it, I have no idea as to what is going on at the University, but, I suppose several of the buildings have been destroyed. Well, at any rate, Germany too has fallen at last. For those of us who happened to have the opportunity to know the great Germany of the past, the Germany that always rose up after sinking down to rock bottom many times, it is difficult to imagine them giving up without a struggle—as an enervated people who cannot accomplish anything. I can say the same thing about France. Or, rather, what I should say is that Europe is not quite yet composed of peoples and nations which have become so antiquated that they are ready to be stored away behind the glass windows of museums. The truly immense problem of a brand-new world looms before us, a world where a new Europe, a new Asia, and a new rest of the world will all be linked together. I am so certain that a second-rate kind of study will prove woefully inadequate for dealing with a challenge of this magnitude, that I know we will be left behind in this whole new development if we allow ourselves to be utterly consumed by the problems that face us right now. The end of hostilities will most certainly provide a great opportunity for change, but somehow I cannot feel that the close of the war is coming any time soon. It is most likely, moreover, that war—as the father of all things—will not simply disappear at the cessation of actual combat. I would not know whether or not it would affect the current fighting, but I think there has to be an absolutely essential kind of study made that would put human beings more in line with their own humanity. We might call this sort of thing "*werden*" (the German original for "development" or "growth"). — And it is also the sort of thing that we constantly—day and night— ought to be making improvements on, despite the difficulties involved.

Please continue your studies in the best of health.

WADA, Minoru

Born January 13, 1922. From the First Higher School, he entered the University, Faculty of Jurisprudence, October 1942. Entered (Naval Training) Corps, December 1943. Died on duty, July 25, 1945, (in an accident) while training as a member of the Kaiten Special Attack Unit.

December 28, 1943

I spotted the *Teidai Shinbun* (*Imperial Universities Newspaper*). And devoured it voraciously, feeling as though I were a student again. It said that the images of those of us who were taken from the middle of our studies and conscripted to fight the war are beautiful. I wonder whether or not this is truly the case.

Until very recently, we were either thinking that we had truly already reached our main goal or, at the very least, that we were looking straight at it. Shortly afterwards, however, and once we more nearly approached what was supposed to have been our grand target, we found that more often than not it was concealed behind a myriad of the little obstacles which surrounded us. It got so that we began to concentrate only on the high points and low points of each day as it came along. It may be far from a satisfactory story, but the truth is that our lives came to center around things that we had to deal with on a day-to-day basis.

All too often arts and culture are totally dismissed as being unimportant, but this only happens when the people who do so have a poor attitude. If they were afforded the grace of *yoyu* (leeway, extra time, composure, etc.) in which to enjoy them, they would probably be immediately converted. Indeed the whole situation exists precisely because the real target of their hatred is not the arts or culture itself but rather the deprivation of the *yoyu* (extra room and time/luxury) which enables people to think about arts and culture.—Simply stated, these same people are quite jealous, and among military personnel their numbers are multiplied.

(The following was written while the author was in training school —during the time of *yobi gakusei* [student reservist/cadetship]) September 24, 1944

I wish to deal with the gap which exists between the military men and the students, and I am drawing my ideas from the last issue of *Kōryō Jihō* (a publication of the First Higher School) that my friend Tanabe let me borrow the other day. Professors Yanaihara and Tachisawa were contributors, as were the dormitory's committee chairman and its other members. With the exception of some sensible fiction by Hiroshi Uda, all the material and essays (written by these students) concerned with literary art were as infantile as though they had been written by middle-school students.

Somehow I could not get my mind around what seemed to be the journal's predominant theme, i.e., its authors' attachment to "things cultural" vis-à-vis the resentment they expressed toward the more practical aspects of life in the contemporary world. I considered all this to be nothing more than a pertinacious—if indeed an irresolute—clinging to traditional things which were hidden behind a mask of sentimentally conservative culture. At the same time, however, I could not bring myself to negate that time of my life when I too had been a student who got indignant or excited over the very same sort of thing. Ever since entering the Navy Corps, I think that I have been successful in maintaining that generally positive attitude towards my world which I have held since my student days.

So far as my basic thinking goes, I think I can assume that, deep inside, there is absolutely no change, even though less than a year's experience of military rules and the military spirit may have been filmed over it. But, at least in my own case, what exactly is that way of thinking, and what does it mean when I now react to a certain ideology in such a different way? Is this progress, or does it mean that, mentally, I am unconsciously wandering about on a promenade reserved for military men? Or is it simply that—with respect to those categories for interpreting things which are peculiar to traditional culture as opposed to today's—I have turned things topsy-turvy?

October 4, 1944

Last evening a transport sailed from here carrying a full load of soldiers. We were waving our hats to them but when I looked at the soldiers through binoculars I noticed that they were all just lined up on the deck, dazed and pale-faced, and that they did not even bother to respond to us.

We continued to raise and wave our hats to send them off, but they never responded—they kept watching the waterway.

October 9, 1944

Here lately I have started to dream dreams about women. At Ōtake, and also at Takeyama, I am certain that I only dreamt either about food or about my home, but things are easier now both physically and psychologically and perhaps the sense of my personal manhood is gradually returning to me. By way of contrast, my appetite is gradually becoming more normal. And now I think that it would be utterly impossible for me now to eat as ferociously as I did when I shocked my mother and younger sister at Ōtake.

The sand in the navigation schoolyard is beautiful. It turns quickly to the color of chocolate when the rain wets it, and the small grains of sand which thinly cover it look like a spread of sugar. When one walks on it, it is never uneven like asphalt or unreliable like ordinary brown soil—it is always gentle and soft and it seems, somehow, to respond to our feet. The drill ground at Ōtake was also exactly like this. Whenever I happened to squat down and gather sand with my hand, I am reminded of the soft and mellow sound of the waves of *Seto* (Inland Sea), about which a friend of mine wrote a poem:

> I plodded on, and on
>> but the sand of Ōtake is still so wet from last night's rain
>> —and it keeps falling

The signal training is almost over. Against a shaded concrete wall outside the window you can make out the darker shadow of a long, slender telephone pole. At this lonely time of the evening it occurs to me that I have never before watched a shadow grow while feeling such emotion: today it seems that my heart has gone back completely to the extra-military world.

After two months of days devoted chiefly to rest, I shall be jumping right into the front line of the war. I am wrapping my usually timid heart and nervous temperament in an *oblaat* (a medicinal wafer) of military spirit. My pain will soon be beginning over the failure, deep in my heart, to have the faith to believe in even a righteous cause. At any rate, my military life for the past four months has only amounted to floating along on the surface of the easiest phase of that life.

(As a member of the Special Attack Corps)[1]

---

[1] Commonly known as *Tokkōtai* or *Kamikaze*. Towards the end of the war, Japan's air strength had diminished to such a point that her leaders had come up with a desperate strategy, i.e., to freight down each plane with as lethal a load of explosives as it could carry, in the hope that the plane might make contact with an enemy ship. According to the Americans' own data, American casualties from such attacks amounted to 16 ships sunk and 185 ships damaged; the successful runs on target was said to be between 1

February 1, 1945

I had my first ride in Kaiten.[2]

I read *Kokoro* (Heart), by Sōseki (Sōseki Natsume, 1867–1916), and also *Jinsei Gekijō* (*Life Theater*), by Shirō Ozaki (a popular novelist, 1898–1964). I have read both books before, but now that I am in this predicament and surrounded by an atmosphere of death, I find myself touched by them more than ever. I even had tears in my eyes! Works of literature and poetry in particular have lately come to appeal to me collectively—not so much as specific works but rather as literature and poetry in general. I realize that, on the face of it, this must seem way off the mark and even a little ridiculous, but how else am I to account for the fact that they—en masse, as it were—affect me so powerfully, even moving me to tears?

I no longer need anything. Consolation and encouragement—particularly if it is to be offered by way of a long-winded, militaristic harangue, or from a speaker who is playing to his audience—are nothing more to me than occasions for anger.

What a cheap and trifling crowd they are!

The things I want most right now are tears, the same tears I cried during my life in peacetime. I wonder whether or not my heart at the

---

and 3 percent. The number of Japanese men killed in action during the course of these special attacks was recorded as 2,527 Navy and 1,388 Army personnel.

Among other "special attack" weapons were the following: *Kaiten* (lit., a turn of good fortune), human torpedoes; *Shin-yō* (shaking ocean), motorboats equipped with explosives; *Ōka* (cherry blossom), human bombs; and *Fukuryū* (lying dragon), which attacked landing-boats from underneath with explosives from the ocean floor.

[2] *Kaiten* (lit., a turn of good fortune, but also connoting a stupendous task, or saving a nation on the verge of ruin): a name given to a human torpedo. This special attack weapon was fashioned by taking a Model 93 torpedo apart and filling the nose portion with an explosive compound. It was operated by a single pilot and, when an enemy vessel was sighted, was launched from a submarine to smash against the target. It was designed in such a way that, once launched, there was no possibility of its returning. However, there were some which were launched from the land and, therefore, possible to return to the base. Apparently, this type was reserved only for Navy Academy graduate members of *Kaiten*.

time, when I look at myself without benefit of a colored glass, was somehow lost. It is almost certain that I will give up my life for my fatherland before this spring is over, but that is no longer something I care about. Now I am simply trying my best to find a way to live this leisurely life that I have now for the first time.

March 26, 1945

Dear Father and Mother, your son, Minoru, is now in a place like this.

Do you remember the red velvet dress that Wakana (a sister) wore, all dressed up for a concert long ago? Well, I remember how that dress was shining in the light, and the ocean is now shining glossily in the sunlight in just the same way. It is a sleepy afternoon. And I am in command of a four hundred-ton steel tugboat. I wear a pair of binoculars around my neck, and sport the green *kikusui* patch (a floating chrysanthemum crest) of our Special Attack Unit on my left arm. We shall be arriving at Saiki (Ōita Prefecture) in an hour or so. The elderly captain of the boat began to doze off. Dear Father, a sub-lieutenant named Miyoshi has died. He failed to clear the bottom of a ship, and crashed. Water came in from the hatch above, and when he was dragged out after some two hours he was dead—his body limp and his face all bloody. When we turned the Kaiten boat upside down, and drained the water from it, I first thought that the seawater was a strange, rusty shade, but I suppose it must have been a mixture of seawater and Miyoshi's blood. —All of this went on in the rain. That evening, the commander and everyone below were drinking. Then a storm suddenly turned up and, around eleven o'clock, two torpedo boats ended up washed ashore. That sobered up everybody and we dashed over there, but it was too late.

March 27, 1945

At 7 p.m. on the 25, the battle reports on Kaiten were released, and it is my understanding that they are referred to as the Shincho Special Attack Unit. Shincho? Who in the world would select such a name at his own discretion and without our knowledge?

April 18, 1945

One more month left. I feel as though I were facing a semester's final exam. I do not think that I would ever be able to spit words out with anything approaching Second-lieutenant N's bombastic style. All his words and phrases are burning with a supreme patriotism. But my cold and dignified heart is prepared to submerge even that to the depth of my innermost feelings. This sort of reserve is of course certainly insignificant at this point in time, and perhaps should be considered unnecessary. For us, however, who at least once upon a time have learned how to think, I feel that all of this is an unavoidable and a heavy burden to carry but, at least in my case, it is only by carrying that burden upon our shoulders that can close the book on my whole life.

"Cold is the people's heart; Okutsuki (a Shinto graveyard) is my home"—Tatsuzō Ishikawa [a novelist, 1905–1985] has a certain female protagonist write these words in *Tenraku no Shishū* (*Collection of Poems of Falling*).[1] Now, at this point in my life, I reflected seriously on my own coldness of heart, and I deeply felt a penetrating sense of loneliness around it. Is it some cowardice on my part which brings on this sort of emotion after I have roused myself with what I thought was courageous excitement? My fellow soldiers have been very kindly concerned over me the past few days, because I look tired. I came to realize that, even if I had to force myself to do it, I had been trying to make some kind of sense out of my impending death. I felt some comfort in coming to see that all things of that sort can be untangled, no matter how complicated they might seem, in the light of one particular emotion—an emotion which has truly and uniquely belonged to the Japanese people over the course of the past three thousand years. And, I have come to feel like gently stroking that coldness which is stuck in the underside of my heart, something that is perhaps unique to me. I feverishly made an opposite angle chart so that I can successfully aim my body at an enemy target.

May 6, 1945

Within this last month of my existence, am I about to come to a conclusion concerning this confusing life of mine? The hands of a sand-clock, which is not quite ready to give out, keep on ticking. I know that precise time at which I am due to attack is the point when I cannot afford to maneuver; even then, though, I sometimes experience private fears.

---

[1] "Falling" in the sense of dropping lower and lower, either morally or else in terms of one's social or occupational status.

Up until now, and just because I was so shallow, I managed to maintain a calm and expressionless front. And now, for the very first time, I am truly at a loss over how to make sense of my past. Impatiently I am struggling to find my true self, that is, without any pretense in my remaining life of just a month.

It already seems to me that I no longer really exist.

I also rode on a torpedo which, without ever floating up, prowled over the ocean floor, and rubbed briskly against it some thirty five meters below. I operated another torpedo that stuck in the sand of the ocean floor, at a depth of thirty meters, inclination at 40 degrees, looking under my shoes at my fellow rider's face. There was another torpedo—when I opened the hatch white smoke suddenly spread over the whole length of the tube because of the high internal pressure—and I felt as though someone had struck me in the face. I have grown into manhood in this squad, and have come to be known as one of "amazing ability," recognized by others as well as by myself. Others may even cry, wondering how I have ever survived this long—that is my life each and every day.

—Notes found inside the boat after *shutsugeki* (sally)—
(The author was carrying this, the record of his very first sally, when he met with the accident which killed him. These notes were discovered later inside the Kaiten boat.)

June 1, 1945

I used to be of an extremely nervous temperament. A variety of unfortunate acts that I had committed in the past never allowed me to fall asleep at night; they also made me rather tentative in my everyday actions. As for other people's acts, however, which I believed to be unfortunate, I took an attitude of withholding even the very slightest forgiveness. As a result those severe words of mine and my conduct, as well as my lack of concern for the people around me, usually proved to be self-defeating and kept me from reflecting on my own faults. In other words, I always held tight to those same ideas of what was right and what was just as were held by Ibsen (Henrik Ibsen (1828–1906); indeed I held to them too emotionally. Therefore, rather than anything material, I hated only metaphysical evil. I think that herein lies the reason for others' misunderstanding of me, and now I recognize that there are many points about which I should be deeply apologetic with regard to the means I took and the methods I used to express them. I was far too emotional as well as stratagem-oriented, and I never took my own qualifications—or lack of them—into account. —This is really the only regret I have with regard to my personal history, aside of course from the fact that the day is fast approaching when I shall have to sacrifice myself in the service of my country.

June 12, 1945

People who cannot put any confidence in human nature ought to be pitied. When we first arrived here on assignment, we spent over a dozen easy days in total idleness. People might perhaps feel that we showed a lot of poise and grace in facing up to the death that was so soon to come, but I would have to say that it was all valueless, for it was just a natural, everyday habit assumed by people without any particular courage, who are being forced to face death.

Our education at the First Higher School was so superb that nothing in the world can be compared to it. I felt such a sense of self-reliance, independence, and indeed peerlessness that I could stand resolutely, tall and alone. If I were to say in a single word, the spirit of the place was "the spirit of *shishi* (a man of integrity, courage and loyalty)." The *shishi*'s spirit is an aggressive one, and the atmosphere of those three years of *Kōryō* (the three year dormitory life of the First Higher School) made me—even as small-minded a person as I was—into a spiritual purist. It also made me able to stand up often to the more powerful people in this world. Now that I am waiting for the enemy like this here in Ulithi (an atoll in the western Caroline Islands), the highway for a supply route to Okinawa, I think of what I learned from those young and receptive patriots, and of the fighting spirit that was rooted in the place, and then I get a firm, quiet feeling in the lower abdomen. Others should not consider me arrogant; it is simply that I am very happy and content.

At night I walked up to the bridge and, off to my right, I spied the Great Dipper. The Southern Cross twinkled on the left, Corona was directly above, and the Milky Way looked like a white cloud.

June 20, 1945   *Kitō* (Ordered to return to the base)

To avoid thinking about life and death through the use of one's abilities to talk convincingly to false phantoms and, similarly, to face up to false, everyday illusions, might seem like something close to transcending these matters, but this is absolutely not the case. We can say that there is a spiritual awakening between life and death only when one is constant about doing his best at self-discipline. —Once reached, this accomplishment is not a fleeting thing.

My whole life has been one of vanity, and it has been also a life of obsequiousness. But for me, as I am, the days of quiet observation which this month provided me will turn out to be a period that provided punctuation to my life in every sense of that term. It has not borne fruit as yet, however.

I recall how at one point, after I had read Shirō Ozaki's *Jinsei Gekijō* (*Life Theater*), I suddenly looked back and realized how full of the "theatrical" my whole life had been (in a sense parallel to that process through which the classical Greek word for a performer on the stage developed into our "hypocrite"). —Even those current views of mine on life and death that I am so proud of might only be another side of that same tendency. A renewed and increased effort in the direction of complete self-examination is in order.

NAKAMURA, Tokurō

> Born October 2, 1918. From the First Higher School, Entered the University, Faculty of Science, Geography Department in October 1942. Entered the barracks in October of 1942. Departed for the Philippines in June 1944 and was missing ever since. (Later reported killed in that area in October 1944.

—Excerpt from his notes while he was in the barracks—
(These were written during his service with the Narashino 9th Unit, Chiba Prefecture. He was a tank soldier at that time, which was the period which separated the rank of Second Class Private from that of Superior Private.)

January 21, 1943
As I was washing a mask, I heard a train whistle. It was strangely long, and sounded as though it were echoing over the mountains. The indigo-blue cloud of sunset, with its shining edge, looked like a crystallized quartz, and was beautiful.

February 20, 1943
The *gakumon*, the pursuit of knowledge, should set the condition of life. That is my cherished contention. Yet, it seems that at the pres-

ent time the exact opposite is the case: *gakumon* is being led about by the condition of life. (Statement by instructing officer Asakawa).

That is absolutely the case, so what in the world is going on? It makes me fearful for the fate of my country.

March 14, 1943

To live is to die and to die is to live: such situations do exist indeed.

*　　*　　*

The idea is to devise some permanent form for transient things: to draw out a divine meaning from tiny things which are insignificant in themselves, and pick out an outline of ideas from natural phenomena. (*Shi to Yūjō* [*Poetry and Friendship*] by Toshihiko Katayama. Published in February 1943).

Oh, I want to be more life-centered!

April 13, 1943

"It is so dangerous, very dangerous indeed, for a single entity—whether it be an individual, or a period (of time), or a nation, or people—to be overwhelmed by the prospect of material wealth. It is one thing to look forward to the road ahead of them and to dream of the future, even to long for eternity and chase immortality: it is quite another to forget that history has to be treated with respect, that room must be left for the due veneration of high ideals, and that all of these things have to be viewed from the proper perspective." (Professor Tachisawa).

April 26, 1943

In the afternoon, I went from Shibuya to my dormitory. I met Mr. Tamaki and heard some recent news: a telegram arrived from Germany about Karl Wils, a friend of mine—he had been killed in action in Stalingrad. I heard that Karl's rank had been that of a Superior Private. I suppose that he too was among those mourned by the playing of (Beethoven's) Fifth Symphony.

Wils's life had already almost been lost on a rocky ledge of Hodaka Mountain; as things turned out, he did not even last four full years afterwards. I am reminded of many things about that evening. I wonder whether, perhaps, he was one of those killed in a tank, his dead body buried in it.

Whatever the situation, it was simultaneously so far away and yet so very seriously similar to my own life.

> (Note: Three years earlier, the author had rescued Karl Wils after the latter suffered a serious mountain-climbing accident on an *iwaba* (a rocky ledge) on Hodaka Mountain in the Northern Japan Alps. The author attended to Karl Wils throughout the night and saved his life.)

April 29, 1943

The lowering of one's intellectual ability. The diminution of intelligence.

Against such things we should struggle with all our might. But, even that would only turn out to be wasted effort!

*   *   *

In a tank, I run westward through the field of Musashino[1]! Zelkova trees (*Zelkova acuminata*) and cedar trees, bamboos and miscellaneous trees . . . and the smells of the field. I smell the aroma of the soybean soup being prepared for the evening meal, mixed with the fragrance of young plant shoots. What a joy that was to recognize those fragrances, however faintly, in the midst of the smoke generated by a lightweight tank. I kept manipulating the gear which operated the tank, hoping all the while that those fragrances and scenes and the sheer joy of being in it would continue endlessly.

May 5, 1943

Patience is by far the most delicate process for the crystallization of life.

The power of poetry is a power which can overcome trials and whatever misfortunes might come along.

I have learned to appreciate the truly great power of poetry.

May 9, 1943   (Sunday)

The University's May Festival has rolled around, and I spent a full day reading books leisurely. One was *Kojin-sho* (a collection of essays) [by Yoshishige Abe, a noted scholar] and another *Shisaku to*

---

[1] Translator's note: Musashino is the name for the plain of the broader Tokyo area, some parts of which, until some fifty years ago, had remained untouched from long ago.

Taiken (*Cogitation and Experience*) [by Kitarō Nishida, a leading philosopher]. A commentary on literature by Junsuke Suita [a scholar on German literature] caught my eye. How poisonous and negative it is. I cannot help but feel disgust and rage from the very bottom of my heart. We are not working to attract sympathy or to get attention from the people.

May 15, 1943

We can so easily become a frog in a well. I cannot always say that there is never a time when we indulge ourselves in easy self-praise or self-satisfaction, or be so perfectly self-contented without really knowing ourselves. Praising Japan's beautiful points and positive qualities, and shedding tears and being generally impressed over our many heroic deeds are natural things to do—but that should not be all we do. We have to situate ourselves within and pay more attention to the big picture. What are the things we truly can be proud of? What should we be proud of? And, again, what do we really mean by pride itself? We have to reflect upon ourselves thoroughly. And we have to reject cheap emotion and self-importance as we would tinware. When I hear prolonged and excessive self-glorification, I want to throw up.

The Japanese people are supposed to be much more modest. Only if we can go quietly about making those great sort of contributions which would be deeply felt in the hearts of all mankind throughout the world, only then will the greatness of the Japanese race brilliantly adorn universal history.

Empty posturing without real strength must be completely rejected. Real strength is not something that can be easily attained—or attained with just an ordinary amount of effort.

Solely because we are the nation which has never been defeated, should we rest on our laurels and do nothing? I am not saying, of course, that to be proud of our country is at all a bad thing. But the issue at point is that, regardless of how bad the defeat a nation suffers or how sad the situation it falls into as a consequence, all that matters is whether or not the people manage to maintain a lively and positive national spirit, and never allow themselves to stumble down the miserable path of defeat. They should be able to exhibit the real strength that rises from the very depths of defeat itself.

When I think along these lines, I feel like going back to reading history. We must search through history, widely and in depth. If we did so, we would never be content to indulge in meaningless self-glorification or self-satisfaction. There is nothing which would endanger a nation more than that sort of "dreaming," and there has never once been a conceited nation that has risen and prospered.

Regardless of how hard we try, we cannot escape from the limitations that history imposes upon us.

May 16, 1943

I am still alive today, but I wonder whether or not it amounts to anything more than that. How lonely it would be merely to survive biologically. —And what utter meaninglessness that would amount to!

May 18, 1943

I heard that an organization called *Bijutsu Hokokū-kai* (Serving the Nation Society for the Arts) was founded. It joins the list of other organizations such as *hōkoku-tai* (serving the nation troop), or *hōkoku-dan* (serving the nation corps), or *hōkoku kai* (serving the nation society) and so on.[2] People seem to think everything will be great if only the term *hōkoku* is used in the beginning of any name. Perhaps people may be thinking it is enough if they just add on "Serving the Nation" to the Society for the Arts too; people may be thinking it is enough if they just keep on painting pictures of war. We should say that they could not be more wrong. They talk out loud and in a grandiose manner without even thinking about what '*hōkoku*' really means. I am both concerned and hopeful that what they are doing will not turn out to be '*bōkoku*' (destroying the nation) rather than '*hōkoku*' (serving the nation).

No matter where I look, I see evidence of the same phenomenon, i.e., an abundance of ritualistic and superficial sycophancy towards us (i.e., the students mobilized for the war). This is a contrived attitude, far from genuine, and it could even become a dangerous situation if we do not soon make a move of our own.

May 20, 1943

I saw a friend today who has never lost the essential quality of his own humanity, even though, and with great courage, he had to fight his

---

[2] All of these refer to the government-sponsored nationalist movement organizations, such as Dai-Nippon Sangyō Hōkoku-Kai (Great Japan Serving-the-Nation Society for Industry), and Dai-Nippon Shōgyō Hōkoku-Kai (the same for Commerce) of 1940, Dai-Nippon Genron Hōkoku-Kai (for speech making) of 1941, and groups called *Hōkoku-dan* or *Hōkoku-tai* organized in each school. (Note: *tai* means corps, *dan* means group, and *kai* means society.)

way through this extremely harsh life.[3] The sight of him provided an immeasurably powerful inspiration for me: I must do my very best to train my mind to be stronger.

I wonder what style of life I should adopt. Hypocrisy and ostentation are qualities that we human beings must regard with the utmost contempt and denounce the most. This is as true, and as internationally so, as that one and one equals two. The sum of one and one is two in Japan, Germany, England or anywhere. It would be impossible, as well as inharmonious, for the sum to be three or four only in Japan.

I will make this my starting point.

August 5, 1943

A copy of the memorial pamphlet honoring my friend Inada was sent to me, and I spent all day reading it. It touched me in a special way and my heart was filled with deep emotion. Each one of our activities —such as marching, class elections, fund-raising campaigns for the Science 4 class—is a dear memory that brings tears to my eyes. How can the meaningfulness of our committee members' lives be put into words? Ah!

It felt as though our hearts had been deeply stabbed and gouged when I learned that, while he was at a sanatorium in Ichikawa, knowing or not knowing that only a very little time was left in his life, he still kept on reading *Fukuso Kansū-ron* (*A Theory on the Functions of Complex Elements*) and *Furansu-go 4-shūkan* (*French in 4-Weeks*), and even wrote some Japanese poems. We must be loyal and true to ourselves until the very last moment of our lives. We must never discard our true duty before we have drawn our last breath.

September 9, 1943

On our way home from maneuvers, Instructor A and myself somehow got involved in a conversation about the current state of education. I was deeply impressed and touched beyond words when I recognized the sincerity of his strong longing towards and great respect for *gakumon* (the pursuit of knowledge), and also of his genuine and intense patriotic concern over the situation in which the nation today finds itself.

Italy's surrender has been reported. How about us?

---

[3] Translator's note: the metaphoric flavor of the original comes through more like "a life of autumn frost and severe sun."

September 12, 1943

In the evening I read *Hakutō* (*White Peach*)[4] in solitude. When I opened the book and put my nose down to catch the scent of paper, I was so deeply affected that tears filled my eyes. I read *Takayama no Kuni Ginkō* over and over. It is a quiet evening and cool autumn breeze grazes my skin.

September 20, 1943

A letter has arrived from my dear friend Mr. Noguchi. What a beautifully calm and quiet tone is carried by every word and every line. In their flawless perfection, the very sound of his most admirable expressions resonates like a silver ring. —Those weapons of war that are "well cared for" shine with a natural beauty, and they will make a difference when the time of danger arrives.

*   *   *

I lay down in the middle of the field. The book, *Kakuritsu-ron* (*Essays on Probability*) made me so very happy—it seemed as though it were hugging me from out of the middle of blue skies and leaden clouds alike.

February 11, 1944

"Fire was burning red in the fireplace. Through a clouded window-glass, the quiet shade of a lamp reflected the quietly dancing snow. A pineapple dish and red tea of the English variety were on the table; they pleased our tongue more than ever. —What a pleasant feeling of tiredness!"

I remember, with the utmost loving longing—like a golden dream —how dusk fell on a particular evening four years ago today. So very well do I remember that day, when the *Sanbon-yari* (Three Spears) Mountain climbing was completed, that I decided today was a good day to pick up a pen again. I pray that this ink will never dry out, and on my part will make every effort to ensure that the prayer is answered. I am also most certainly aware of how important it is to read; nevertheless, I feel it is even more important to write. I think, too, that the matter of just exactly where the essence of writing is is a very important issue. Someone has said that "To write is to be deeply rooted in the

---

4 By Mokichi Saito, 1882–1953.

broad and vast love for human beings"—something like that. Well said, indeed.

Upon reflection, it seems to me that I must face and answer the question as to why I wanted to start writing again. Merely writing notes to show to others, or keeping a diary with the intention of showing it to others, are most certainly writings of no value; in fact, they are definitely of a low order and, in a way, merely a distorted sort of scribbling. Time after time I get this very strong urge to write—just a simple need to get things down on paper. It has also been my experience, however, that again and again and for a variety of reasons, those same urges disappear like bubbles, and without becoming actual letters. Lately I have come to think of this as a regrettable situation, even though I do not really know the reasons for it.

February 13, 1944

I finished reading *Kūkan to Jikan* (*Espace et le Temps*) by Émile Borel. I read it with great interest, which is a rare thing for me these days.

February 14, 1944

Once again I read *Doitsu Senbotsu Gakusei no Tegami* (*Letters of the Fallen German Students*) [Japanese translation of selected pieces from *Kriegsbriefe gefallener Studenten*, compiled after WWI by Prof. Philipp Witcop of Freiburg University, and published in Japanese by the Iwanami Publishers as an Iwanami New Library book]. The book continues to be rewarding no matter how many times you read it, and it is especially impressive to read here. These writers are sincerity itself, and happy were they who, in a trench and under the light of a candle, read the Bible, read Goethe, cited Hölderlin's [Johann Christian Friedrich, 1770–1843] poetry, and longed to listen to Wagner's music. They were fortunate, because they did. . . .

One notation is particularly noteworthy: "Not a single insulting word about the enemy was found in a letter recovered from the body of a fallen soldier."[5]

---

[5] In a letter of Hugo Muller, contained in the *Kriegsbriefe gefallener Studenten* (*Letters of the Fallen German Students*), translated by Kenji Takahashi, was the following: "I am enclosing a French soldier's postcard . . . . This postcard was taken from the dead French soldier's pocket notebook. . . . What surprised me was that there was not a single insulting word about us (i.e., German soldiers) . . . ."

I envy the strength hidden within the German race that could have produced such serious, even great students. I have come to realize that the fine qualities of the Japanese military—such as their transcendent conquest of the fear of death itself, their courageous charges, etc.,—are not necessarily unique to Japan. I cannot help but to renew my belief and trust in the true strength of the really genuine and lofty type of rationality.

Generally speaking, the descriptions of Christmas are particularly beautiful. When we were young, too, Christmas was a world of *märchen* (German term for fairy-tale). I feel so sorry for the Japanese children who do not have too much of *märchen* in the first place, and even more so in light of today's trend towards losing even more of it.

February 18, 1944

Completed my reading of *Bunka Chiri-gaku* (*Cultural Geography*) by Tarō Tsujimura, and published by Iwanami. I felt the vastness of his *gakumon* (the pursuit of knowledge), its degree of difficulty, and his limitless hopes for pursuing his subject further. I should like to gain strength by thinking of Mendel's [Gregor Johann Mendel, Austrian botanist, known for his Mendel's Law, 1822–1884] words:

"Stay alert! Soon my time will come."

February 22, 1944

This is the day I learned about the death of Professor Mitani [Takamasa Mitani, a legal-philosophy scholar and professor at the First Higher School, 1889–1944]. Such a sorrow for Japan! A giant star has fallen. As if looking at a shooting star. . . .

We were almost the very last students of Professor Mitani, and I was lucky to be one of them. My association with him began when I was in my first year, with his lecture on legal economy. I always chose a seat in the very first row, exactly below the lecture desk, for listening to his lectures. It was then I learned about Schweitzer [Albert Schweitzer, Alsatian medical missionary, noted theologian, organist, and philosopher, 1875–1965] and Stirner [Max Stirner, German anarchist, philosopher, 1806–1856] for the first time. Prof. Mitani's lectures on "knowledge and faith," "on Prof. Iwamoto," and his memorial address at the funeral service for Professor Iwamoto—were delivered with deep emotion; I can remember his powerful spirit.

On the 17th I learned of Professor Eijiro Kawai's passing. An individual's great personal character is not something that comes about just because one wishes it to come about. Airplanes and ships can be manufactured. The great personalities—both of the past and in our own time—are treasures not only for Japan but for all humanity. The more such treasures a nation has, the greater that nation is.

The experience of internal pain helps to develop a great character; conversely, a nation that has not experienced real pain can never be called great.

March 1, 1944

In many senses I have not yet touched the core of life, and I must strive to be more genuine and much more single-minded.—And it would be all right to have more dreams.

March 3, 1944

To get something is a joy, but to give is an even greater one. Those who know the joy of receiving something are fortunate, but those who know the joy of giving are even more so.

March 5, 1944   (Note: the day General Doihara came to the unit for inspection)[6]

One must be good and always stay good even when placed in the midst of others' viciousness and the cruelty of fate itself. In the middle of many painful disagreements, he should never lose his gentleness and kindness, and must undergo such experiences without allowing the opposition to touch the treasure of his inner heart. I wish to remain mild even in the most severe fights, remain good in the middle of evil people, and to be tranquil even in the middle of war.

To live undiscovered and without being taken notice of by others—how potent and powerful such a life is! In contrast, those people with evil qualities cover the earth and, soaking themselves in the sun, steal the social positions and happiness of others—those evil ones who might best be described as the living dead!

There will be no prosperity for a nation if and when the longing for the truth is lost.

---

[6] Inspections, or *ken-etsu*: higher ranking officers conducted on-site inspections in such areas as living up to military rules, the state of academic military training, participation in field experiences, etc. An inspection required everyone to be at their best and most attentive. In the military training in the college and higher school setting, it was also called *saetsu*.

March 12, 1944

Poland is a country whose history is full of ups and downs. It fell in the eighteenth century. But it revived after the First World War. Shortly thereafter, though, it was recently once again swallowed up by Germany. It is a nation with endless rises and falls. The same is true with Italy, . . . and it is also a nation that undergoes frequent transformation. However, the glorious existence of those heroes and heroines whom Poland has given birth to—such names as Chopin, Madame Curie, and others come to mind—is a fact that people around the world cannot either ignore or erase from history. So too the forebears of modern Italy—Dante and Copernicus (a Pole actually), as well as Galileo and Da Vinci—they are all cultural treasures commonly shared by the whole of the human race. The contributions one leaves behind cannot under any circumstances be denied. We could say that the greatness of a nation depends upon the production of people sufficiently talented to provide the impetus for enriching the foundation of human life. No matter what fate the future may hold for Japan, we were born with the fate to stand up and carry it. We must not restrict our striving to mere pleasure and ease, for, no matter which beautiful flower or delicious fruit we are concerned with, its root can only be cultivated through suffering and persevering.—I must not die.

March 16, 1944

I heard someone calling me and stuck my neck out from inside the tank. A voice said:

"What do you think, Nakamura? The moon is out. —It's mystic, isn't it?"

As I looked out, the red half-moon had just risen above the woods, at the left end of a field that was now all brightened. As I rolled along inside the slow-moving vehicle (i.e., tank) I felt so simultaneously strange and happy. Power lines were moving up and down in front of the moon. And for some reason I could not help but be reminded of Wilde's *Salome* [Oscar Wilde, English poet and playwright, 1856–1900]. It was probably about four o'clock in the morning when, having returned to the base, I finally hit the bed.—It had been such a moving evening that I thought it would be a shame to sleep.

March 27, 1944

What is really essential is *jissen* (actually doing something). But only slogans and speeches come first and quickly—and how rich they are in flowery words and beautiful phrases! The current situation, at once so remote from both *jitsugen* (realization/actualization) and *jissen* (actually doing something), is truly disgusting. It makes me afraid to use the words that should be used.

Where or in what can the meaningfulness of life be found? Can it be found? Untidy brain! The springtime of life that is lost! One second runs into another and the flow of time does not rest for a moment. Do you know about *Urashima Tarō* (an old Japanese folk tale about a man who saved a sea turtle one day, and as a reward the latter invited him to a sea palace where he was totally unaware of the passage of time)? Well, then, what should we do?

I have felt in recent days that I am not more than merely "alive." The I who is only "being alive" is of almost equal value, though not quite, as the I who is "being dead." Lately I have been pondering over many immoral acts that, in the past, I consciously or unconsciously committed. There are some which can be redeemed: there are some which cannot be redeemed. When I think of these things I feel sad. But I cannot stop thinking about them just because.

April 3, 1944

I was standing at the front gate, and I did something bad. The fact is that I displayed a despicably bureaucratic attitude—a sort of arrogance.

A certain boy urinated near the gate, and I chided him for that behavior. When I looked at the boy, pale-faced and runny-nosed, I myself, who was doing the chiding, felt very sad. Now and then this bureaucratic arrogance shows up in my personal attitude and, whenever it does, another side of me despises it. At those times I inevitably feel an increased sense of self-condemnation.

April 27, 1944

My head is filled with things that I want to think and am going to think—that I must think. This makes me very happy.

May 8, 1944

There is a single wisteria vine, hung with beautiful flowers in full bloom, and I kept my eyes on it. I saw in my imagination the wisteria tree which stands in front of the biology classroom, and that must be in full bloom right now. —I wonder who are now lying under its shade.

May 12, 1944

Attended by an unusually deep emotion, I finished reading *Alt Heidelberg* (a German play by Meyer-Förster, dealing with young love and student life at Heidelberg University). I am extremely happy that I was able to have my own Heidelberg.

May 13, 1944

Finished reading *Wakaki Veruteru no Nayami* (*Leiden des jungen Werthers*) [by Johann Wolfgang von Goethe, 1774]. The process that led to his death could not help but touch my heart so deeply. I wonder whether or not I have been lying to myself lately. I wonder whether or not I am too satisfied with easy compromise. I wonder whether or not my sharp and uncompromising sense of justice has been numbed. It is frightening—truly frightening.

It counts for nothing just to be kept alive. The thing is to live!

It is better that we wait, though.

May 26, 1944

Oh! I heard the sound of cascades today. I heard the symphony that permeates deeply into the woods of Narashino.

June 5, 1944

To my Dear Father and Mother:

I shall never forget your *on* (great favor) in bringing me up, over such a length of time, to where I am today—and through all sorts of pains and difficulties. Moreover, I have never done anything in return for that great favor. Please forgive me for my numerous *fukō* (lacks of filial piety). The more I think about this, the more deeply do I feel my repentance.

I wish I could close my life in the ice of the South Pole, or at the bottom of a Himalayan glacier, or atop an ice-wall, or, if none of these, buried under the Turkistan desert. But the god of destiny did not thus favor me.

Everything has been a tragedy, but I also thought of how true it is, as Akutagawa [Ryūnosuke Akutagawa, 1892–1927] has also remarked, that "when we become parents and have children, the tragedy of life has already begun." I pray for blessings upon my unfortunate Father and Mother.

(Note: It was on this day, June 5, that suddenly the author learned that he was to be sent to the front line two days later.)

June 20, 1944   8 o'clock in the morning

(This is the last letter he sent. After having been suddenly ordered to the front line, he wrote this to his parents from Moji en route to his new assignment.)

In Moji City   Tokurō

To my dear Father, Mother and Younger Brother:

Everything was so sudden, and, moreover, it all happened the way it did due to the very tiniest of fate's ironies. But I am not particularly surprised. At least I felt fortunate to be able to see Katsuro (his younger brother), even for an hour. Actually, by that time I was already supposed to have embarked, in which case I could not have seen anyone.

For a variety of reasons, I had to spend more than ten days at an old inn with broken roof tiles, in a pitiful town of Moji that was all weathered by smoke and dirt. Probably you may have already read in the newspaper that I will be sailing off in a few days, leaving many and very special memories behind. Had I known your phone number, I might have been able to phone you and talk for a bit, might even have had an opportunity to visit, but I suppose that this too is a factor of fate.

(Note: At about this same time the author's parents were evacuated from Tokyo to Yamanashi for safety's sake.)

I certainly do not know where we are headed for next. Of course it is sure to be at one of those fronts on which the fighting is most intense. I assume that, at least most probably, I shall not be able to write you a letter for a while—(perhaps for a considerable length of time). Just by coincidence, my friend Takamura[7] is going to be with me; and in whatever situation we may find ourselves, I think we will be able to console each other and make our hearts richer for it. It is regrettable that I did not happen to have the books that I really wanted to keep with me, but nothing can be done about that. However, I did bring several other books with me.[8]

Upon my departure, up to the very moment I left from the barracks-gate, those seniors and *senyū* (comrades-in-war), who for the

---

[7] Mr. Takamura was at the First Higher School, Science-2 (Science, German language concentration), 3rd year student at that time.

[8] *Kaesaru-Garia Senki (Caesar's Commentaries on the Gallic War)* (Iwanami Bunko), *Doitsu Kokumin ni Tsugu (Reden an die Deutsche Nation)* by Johann Gottlieb Fichte [1762–1814] (Iwanami Bunko); *Gēte Shirureru Ōfuku Shokan-shū (Collection of Correspondence between Goethe and Schiller)*; "Carossa: Rumaenisches Tagebuch," "Mountain Essays"; *Saikin Sekai-Shi Nenpyō* (Most Recent World History Chronological Table); several Iwanami Zensho books, etc.

time being are remaining behind, took care of my every need. Unlike classmates at school, the only bond of unity that came to exist among these *senyū* friends of mine had been formed by a fleeting accident of fate, and I did not even know the home addresses of many of them— indeed, of most of them. Very probably I will never see most of them ever again. Nevertheless, the kindness they showed me, so beautiful even in its smallest manifestations, and so many other sincere expressions of their goodwill will never leave my heart all the rest of my life. That reminds me of the night before I entered the barracks, when, and in a very beautifully thoughtful way, filled with kindest thoughts, a classmate of mine from Science-4, Mr. Hatta, made me a gift of ten-yen. He is currently studying at the Second Faculty of Engineering, Civil Engineering Department. I would appreciate it very much if you would not forget to thank him for me.

I did write both to Professor Tsujimura [professor and head of the Geography Department, Tokyo Imperial University] and Director Abe [Yoshishige Abe, a prominent scholar who then headed the First Higher School]. I regret that I was unable to write to Mr. Aramata, who has been the professor in charge of my class since my first year as well as the moderator of the mountain-climbing club, and also to Mr. Toyama of the First Middle School. So, please convey my warmest regards when you have a chance. I think that perhaps I shall have an opportunity to see Mr. Morris [former lecturer at the First Higher School] again, but if anything should happen to me (and of course that probability is high), please tell him how it happened and also how I have been getting along since I last saw him; also, there is a letter from me to Mr. Morris (currently in Katsuro's keeping) that I would ask you to pass along to him. Should he not visit Japan, you will find his home address in London written down in the address section of my latest diary.

As for myself now, I have not quite regained tranquillity in my heart. That is simply because I am unsettled about the whole thing, and I cannot blindly accept it either. Is there anything more meaningless than for a human being—especially if he amounts to anything at all and has his own personality—to be ordered about at will, with total disregard for his thoughts and impulses, and without receiving due respect, by the whimsical brain cells of a certain unreasonable stranger, and to become a mere mathematical function? Whatever happens, I have no wish to dwindle into something like a piece in a chess game.

At any rate, I am keenly desirous of returning to the classroom as soon as possible and doing my best to accomplish my original mission. While in this current predicament, I cannot help but feel a strong regret over the fact that my youth is being stolen away little by little. The work that I was going to carry out is something of such significance that, I believe, it is reasonable to say, not even one other person in Japan would be willing to tackle it. Moreover, and considering the advantages I had, I do not believe that there are many people, even in the whole world, who could do the work. Although it is certainly not my aim, I firmly believe that the completion of my study would bring truly great honor and glory to Japan's position in the world, far more than would the winning of a war or the occupation of an island or cities.

Of course it is needless to say that, even for me to have advanced as far as I have, I owe so much to Prof. Tsujimura, but, at the same time, Mr. Morris's influence cannot be disregarded. He taught me what a true human being, and the human race itself, has to do. I feel too that it was he who taught me what *gakumon* (the pursuit of knowledge) really is. I cannot forget the words he said to me, "Devote yourself to science!" was what he said on a certain evening, as I sat in front of him, stirring red tea with a Tibetan silver spoon, in a room with a Tibetan fresco hanging.

> Note: Mr. Morris was a lecturer at the First Higher School, and at the time of the publication of this book, was a BBC commentator in London.

*   *   *

So long as the present situation prolongs itself, I am utterly concerned with the future of my homeland. Just saying that Japan is a very unique country does not exempt it from the usual rules of history. To think so would be as comical as someone who boasted that his body was specially made and therefore not subject to the rules of modern biology. Even assuming that we will win the war, it is most certain that we must give serious thought to what kind of a future condition, and for a long time to come, today's situation will usher in. History will decide as to who was really a true patriot, and who was not. As for myself, I don't care whether I receive meritorious medals or not, I shall be satisfied if the value placed upon me in the permanence of history is that of a truly patriotic person.

Should you hear that I have "died," please do not believe that death came from an enemy bullet, and against my will. For when the battle situation gets extremely harsh, and when it is time, I have accepted the idea of taking my own life, and indeed intend to do so. I would, however, like to believe that this will not be necessary, even though the odds are very much against me.

*   *   *

Please allow Katsurō to study to his heart's content. I think you can trust him and let him do what he needs to do. I cannot help but think that I do not want him to experience the loneliness of having to worry so much about getting a book, or some such matter. In fact, the more I think about him, the more pity I feel for him—because the current situation is too cruel and restricted for study. I think it is so unfortunate. The other day, when he came to see me for the last time, I talked to him, under the supervision of an officer, in a very businesslike manner in the officers quarters: I thought he had tears in his eyes while he was looking down and painstakingly taking copious notes on what I was saying. I felt so sympathetic and sorry for him.

Already it is getting dark. Now I have to get ready and take care of a lot of details connected with the departure. I shall leave in good health. Please take really good care of yourselves, and do not worry about me. (Just in case of my death,) I left my fingernails and hair for you at the regiment the very last minute before I left.

To Katsurō:

I have written down a variety of things in another place. When I went out on supervised leave today for the last haircut, unexpectedly I was able to get some books at a nearby bookstore. I am carrying them with me just for pleasure. These are the titles:

1. *Gēte Shirureru Ōfuku Shokan-shū* (*Collection of Correspondence between Goethe and Schiller*), vol. 1.

2. *Bungaku to Bunka* (*Literature and Culture*).

3. *Keisei-teki Jikaku* (*Self-Consciousness in Formation*).

4. *Sanseidō Saikin Sekai-shi Nenpyō* (*Most Recent World History Chronological Table*).

As far as the things I asked you about the other day go, I know it is bothersome, but please take care of them steadily.

P.S. Because of the government limit placed on traveling, my friends in Dormitory North No. 27 will also have trouble getting to any place west of Kōfu. If so, I think that the only places they can climb will be Oku-Chichibu (interior of Chichibu), centering around Enzan, or the southern part of the Japanese Alps from Kōfu. Perhaps the former could be best utilized. When they stop by our home, would you please take care of them for me? Perhaps treat them to milk, or whatever, and to their hearts' content. I would sincerely appreciate your doing this favor for me.

UMIGAMI, Haruo

> Born March 20, 1921. From Shizuoka Higher School, entered the University, Faculty of Economics, October 1942. Entered the barracks in December 1943. Killed in action, January 9, 1945, in Lingayen Bay, the Philippines.

—My Will[1]—

Death is truly life's deepest abyss, and it must always be kept in any person's heart. I would think, however, that it is imperative—when one is actually facing it—for this focus to be renewed and reinforced.

As I look back over the twenty-some years since I was first given life on this earth, I see that I have been showered with the greatest and most loving favors that heaven and earth had to offer, but also that I have not done anything in particular in return for all that.

For the sake of everything that existed only for me, I do not wish to die in vain. I shall walk deliberately and single-mindedly along the path of requiting all the kindnesses and favors I have received.

November, 1943   Haruo Umigami

—(Last Writing)—

(The author's last writing, jotted down in pencil on a piece of memo paper just before he left on a sortie, January 1945, Luzon Island)

To my Dear Father and Mother:

In high spirits and good health, I am heading out to my assigned position. (In spite of everything,) Haruo is and has been truly a student after all—in every sense of the term.

Haruo

---

[1] Translator's note: This will is written in the classic literary style.

MATSUYOSHI, Masatsugu

Born December 1, 1923. From Yamaguchi Higher School, entered the University, Faculty of Jurisprudence, October 1942. Killed in action, May 11, 1945, in Okinawa, as a member of the Special Attack Forces.

—Miscellaneous Poems on My Hometown—

Sitting behind the row of houses along the shore of a cove,
    the mountains stand tall.

In the mandarin orange field the oranges are ripening
    and I could see them clearly at a distance.

—Effusion of Thoughts—

The warmth of the compassion of the people at home
    I feel ever so deeply, particularly as I am (in the
    predicament of)
        leaving for the battlefield.

Even should my living body be shattered,
    till I leave this world
    I shall never forget the compassion of my compatriots.

FUKAZAWA, Tsuneo

Born September 28, 1918. From Urawa Higher School, entered the University, Faculty of Natural Science, Department of Geology in April 1939, and graduated in December 1941. Entered Naval Training Corps, January 1942. Killed in action in the sea near the Philippines, July 17, 1944.

—Thoughts—

The fact that I was born into this family and that you did so much for me is my greatest good fortune, and the more I think about it the more grateful I am.

I am overwhelmed with shame for not having done anything, even in the slightest way, to return on that (all that you did for me). Now that

I am about to give up my life, I hope that your hearts will at least be comforted by the direction of my thoughts. As usual, I am not disturbed by the fact that I have to die; in fact there are some things which I will be able to do when I die which I would not be able to do were I still living:

I shall protect people, our home, and our country.

Well, I bid you good-bye and hope that you will be well. —There are also a lot of things that one cannot do unless he/she were still living.

(*Tanka* poems composed while he was working on
a surveying ship in the front line of the war)

On a dazzling and glaring sea, faraway
   a coconut floated off into the distance.

We could see nothing for several days but sea and sky,
   although we kept moving forward—and ever forward—
      with men on watch both in the tower and at the stern.

The wake behind our ship is slightly bright and reminds one of
   the Milky Way,[1]
      and there are also some gleaming things—perhaps noctilucae bugs.

The mountains and the island itself are hidden by the rain:
   only our mother ship floats brightly in the rainbow.

We keep on and on, and still the gate of the rainbow remains at
   the same distance,
      but the island is at last becoming larger.

Two large ships moving parallel in the middle of the ocean,
   we entrusted our bodies to a huge rolling swell of the sea.

He is a man with four wives of a certain Chinese tribe
   who is growing old alone in a foreign land.

---

[1] The original Japanese word is *Ginga* (Silver River).

An elderly interpreter was touching the grass on a mound
   while noting that there were only two of us Japanese.

There was a Japanese grave on a wisteria-covered rocky
   mountain,
         though I thought it was too far away to see.

I am carrying a casket down this mountain path where
   lauan trees grow,
         because I wanted to show its northern end
            to my friend who has passed away.

The comfort ladies, who are playing around and blowing water
   on the factory workers,
         are also a thousand *ri* away from home.
         (1 *ri* = 2.44 miles)

ISE, Teruo

> Born August 4, 1923. From the Sixth Higher School, entered the
> University, Faculty of Jurisprudence, October 1943. On January 7,
> 1945, while en route from Taiwan to mainland Japan, contact with
> his plane was lost.

January 25, 1944   (Cloudy, light rain, slightly cold)
   Midwinter exercise. The first group leaves the unit. The bayonet-
fencing drill which had been scheduled for this morning has been cancelled. Those who were being shipped out today are making the final
disposition of their personal effects, while those who will be staying on
cleaned up the camp. Perhaps because, despite a cold, I took part in the
midwinter exercises, I developed a noticeable fever today and had an
awful coughing spell. My whole body was feeling terribly languid. I
want to be completely recovered before I leave the unit and I want to
go in high spirits, but I was down all day today and felt miserable. My
five *sen'yū* (war-time friends)—Kunishige, Takeshi Onishi, Miyai,
Yonemoto, and Matsunaga—quietly left us this evening in a light rain.
Those who were seeing them off were all filled with emotion, as were
those who were actually leaving. Some were even sobbing, and altogether it was a lonelier parting than I had anticipated.

Today we said goodbye to friends with whom we have shared the same fate, even though for only a month and a half; we ate together in the same mess, and shared our labor and pain. Our fate must be repeated in that we shall soon have to part from some others who are still here. Miyai and Yonemoto are such attractive and lively people that they were looked up to as sources of strength in our Third Training Unit. So now my five *sen'yū*, Takeshi Ōnishi, Kunishige, and the others, with whom I trained, and who hung their hammocks alongside mine, are gone. As a result, our training unit has suddenly became a very lonely group; and I feel especially so. My dear friends, you must now be riding on a train now en route to some faraway northern country. —Please stay well, my dear friends.

I thought that perhaps there would be an announcement for the rest of us today, but nothing came. It has been such a tension-filled day, but perhaps some word will come tomorrow. The day was filled with a lot of things which, because of my bad cold, I am not in the mood to write much about just now. I received a package from home just after we had taken down our hammocks. In it I found a *sennin-bari haramaki* (a band to wrap around the stomach, with "a thousand stitches [by a thousand women]"), which must be the product of my mother's and my older sister's hard work. Also included were a variety of medicines such as Asutamu, Sumairu (name of a Japanese medicine), and other digestive medicines, for which I am most appreciative. I opened an envelope in my hammock and the first letter I took out had Kōjirō's calligraphy on it. He wrote "*Ganbare!* (Hold out. Do your best!)" in a truly valiant manner. As a result of my coaching, his calligraphy is of such quality that it deserves a grade of three-circles (grade A). There was also a drawing of *Hinomaru* (the Japanese national flag of the rising sun) which, for a first grader, was also exceptionally well done. Dear Kōjirō, *Ganbare!* Please agree to study hard. His letter written in *katakana* syllables was also enclosed. It said: "I want to see you, my older brother. I am talking to your picture. Please eat your rice-cakes and candies whenever they are served to you. . . ." Each letter is so irresistibly lovely, and his sentiments and longing for me were so genuine that I could do nothing to prevent tears from falling.

The last thing that came out of the envelope was a letter from my mother. Mother's letter was completely unexpected, inasmuch as I had never received even a single letter from her before, or had never seen her write anything at all before. Yet now, and just out of love, she is so kind as to write to me. I am deeply moved and so grateful to her. Her words as they appear on a piece of paper are faltering, just like those of a child, and each individual letter is so innocent and simple. Yes, this is indeed my mother's writing.

"Do not worry about your father and mother, and just do your duty as best you can. Believe in *Konpira-sama* (Kumbhira) because he is the guardian deity of seafarers," she wrote. Tears fell like spring water and I am choked up: my whole body was shaking. This precious love of mother's! Her love is so brave.

"Mother! This undutiful and unfilial child swears, right now, to follow through on what you have taught me." —I was so happy that I could not fall asleep in my hammock.

NAKAO, Takenori

> Born March 31, 1923. From Fukuoka Higher School, entered the University, Faculty of Jurisprudence, April 1942. Conscripted and entered the (Naval Training) Corps, December 1943. Killed in action, May 4, 1945, in the sky over the southwestern Pacific, as a member of Shinpu Special Attack Force, Suishin Unit.

(A letter to Mr. Fumio Yanagiura)

December 7, 1943

Dear Mr. Yanagiura:

I picked up a pen with the intention of writing a letter as the last "visit" from the "*shaba*" (the land of the living, i.e., in this case, the world outside the military); but thousands of words overflow from my heart and I am lost as to what to write. After having returned to Kashii (in Fukuoka City) on the 4th, I read your letter(s) and telegraph(s). I feel terrible and apologetic as I think of you, on the evening of the 28th, trying to find me, searching for me in the gathering dusk of the Kashii train station.

You must have seen continuous and endless trails of footprints on the beautiful sandy shore of Mei-no-hama or Shingu Beach (beaches in Fukuoka City), have you not? I think there was a poem, by Tōson (Tōson Shimazaki, 1872–1943) or someone else, that described such a scene. I feel as though those several strings of footprints which intersected each other there were made by ourselves. We do not know where they begin and where they end, or where they might cross and where they might part again—there is something so impermanent and so sad about the footprints on a beach.

Even though the prints were to be erased by the action of the waves, we would still be able to sense the powerful and reassuring steps, taken one after the other, of the person who made those prints. When I recognize the powerful walk of the person who visited that heap of sand and then left, I feel encouraged. It is indeed true that we do not know either the past or the future; when I stand firmly in the present, however, I feel the power that fills my own legs. I also recall a letter from Katō in which he wrote that "We must walk forever: we must continue to walk forever."

Takenori Nakao

(From his last letter, the day before his first sally, April 28, 1945)

At the send-off party, I was both encouraged by others and also encouraged myself. I am a very lucky man indeed. An insignificant[1] person as I am, I have nothing that I could contribute to others, and yet others have treated me with genuine kindness. I can now leave to fight the war with a courage and happiness which are more than I deserve.

I have nothing more to offer at this point except my prayers for your good health.

I have left behind the diary in which I wrote down my everyday thoughts. I may not have accomplished much, but I pushed on with my heart's desire to live clean and strong, and, as I look back, I am pleased to see that I have not done anything ugly or dirty.

SAWADA, Yasuo

> Born November 29, 1922. From the First Higher School, entered the University, Faculty of Jurisprudence, October 1442. Entered the (Navy) Corps, December 1943. Killed in action, May 1945, in the skies over mainland Japan.

---

[1] Translator's note: a commonly used standard expression to be modest. However, in this case, it is assumed to be an error in copying when this collection was compiled: the literary meaning of the character, as printed, which is out of use in recent decades, is "broad, faraway, appearance of a huge body of water." (m.y.)

(A letter to a friend, Ms. K)
December 15, 1944 Cloudy
Dear K:

Look at how beautiful the evening stars are these days! Do you not think that each one of them is whispering something? When I am feeling sad, those stars look as though they too are sharing the same sadness: when I am feeling joy, they look as though they are sharing the same joy. Do you not agree? I suppose that the stars are so beautiful because their job is to look only at those who are in love.

It has been a year since we parted. A one-year anniversary comes around quickly, doesn't it? There is an expression which runs to the following effect: "the one who leaves drifts farther and farther from our thoughts" (i.e.: "Out of sight, out of mind"). Until recently this had certainly been true in my own case. The dreams each and every night of nothing but you and the sweet and pleasant daydreams I indulged in shortly after leaving Osaka were with each passing day gradually breaking down.

But all this changed dramatically on a very recent Sunday when, once again, I reread all the letters that you have sent me since we parted. Between the conventional lines you wrote, which when I first received those letters I might very well have read without paying particularly close attention, I found something that touched my heart deeply. Then, and for the first time, I felt with my bare conscience the radiance and glitter of your true heart and genuine love.

When I close my eyes and quietly reflect upon the past I realize that, all the while we were seeing one another, I had been building a kind of ditch which separated us. There was a constant struggle in my heart between the emotion that urged me to destroy that ditch and the rationality which desperately wanted to defend it, even unto death— not to speak of the social constraints imposed on me from all sides. I thought long and hard about a way to deal with—and to solve—my dilemma, but in the end I parted from you without having found any solution to that struggle in my heart. I think that this is the reason for what I said and for the way I behaved throughout our last evening together.

I can see now that I lacked both the strength necessary to make decisions and the sensitivity to accept and understand your taking our love a step further. But the odd thing is that, while I actually did perceive what was going on, I also deliberately numbed my nerves for fear of being controlled by something outside myself. In other words, I was fooling myself.

Truly I have never felt my love for you as powerfully as at present. Simply by saying this I am able to become bound to my true heart's feelings and rid myself of all sorts of obstacles which bound me in the past; by saying it I can now lay claim to integrity, even though I am ashamed of my old attitudes. Once again I have begun to dream continuously of you, though this time with different emotions and in an importantly different way. I do not think this feeling will ever change for the rest of my life. —This is my genuine heart!

I am not the sort of man who can easily fall in love with a woman but soon finds someone else to take her place. I think that you too have that same quality. I would think the fact that we are linked as tightly as we are must mean that we are united forever. My life will probably be a very short one but if it is at all possible, and assuming that you would permit me, I am deeply desirous of continuing to make this feeling of mine a reality.

So it is that I deeply regret our last evening together. Please forgive me, I beg you, by thinking that all my actions and words at that point in time were attributable to something demonic in my heart which was binding and numbing my conscience. —Now I am once again filled with the powerful desire to embrace you.

Of course my desire cannot be fulfilled through my own selfishness, but unless there is a good reason which makes it impossible to realize it, I will—absolutely—embrace you and kiss you.

(A letter to Ms. K)
January 7, 1945   (Sunday)   A clear day
My Dear K:

Greetings. Thank you so much for your letter, and I am so glad that you are as well as always. In spite of the fact that things are so scarce nowadays because of this horrible war we are involved in, I trust that you had a pleasant New Year in your heart. I had a nice New Year too, but emotionally it was so very different from a year ago.

Very seldom do we actually act out the things that are in our minds, or do things the way they ought to be done. I am powerfully reminded that, as is usual in this world, everything cannot go the way we wish it to. What I wrote in my previous letter are my true feelings without any hint of falsehood, and also my hopes and desires. I am also thinking that my love is a truly beautiful love which will never change.

Should what I wrote in that letter be possible and ever comes true, then this world will truly be a dreamland and a heaven. All sorts of circumstances, however, are preventing that from happening. I have mentioned all this to you before, and I think you have a general grasp of the situation. Our hopes of and desires for marriage are genuine, and it would certainly be the right thing to do in a nation of gods, but I am afraid that it may not be possible in this world of men.

I can say with all sincerity that I am not asking for your flesh. A woman's body is no more necessary to me than it is to other men—I have not sunk that low. I always wanted to respond to the tolling of the bell that is your beautiful soul—to the sound of your heart. It is true that one's soul cannot be separated from the physical body, but please do not think that just because I wanted your heart that I also lusted after your body.

Just listening to the voice of your soul will be enough for me, because I know that bodily desires are selfish. You too, while you await the time for our physical union, will meet the miserable fate of hoping for something which will never come about. It is because I love you that I must tell you simply to give up the idea of being united with me physically, and advise you to choose someone else. I realize how hurtful this must be, but I dare to say it because I do love you.

Finally, let us—you and I—continue our beautiful relationship for the rest of our lives, realizing both the dream we had and the beautiful platonic love and friendship we currently enjoy. With a prayer for your happiness I am ready to set my pen down, adding only that my love for you is exactly as I described it in my last letter, and that it will remain so forever—even through eternity.

Soon I shall be called to the battlefield.

In the final analysis, I was always fated to end up this way, and perhaps things turned out for the best after all. So far as my own emotions are concerned, all of my anxiety is gone. Still, the fact that I could not have done more to help her is the deepest regret of my life. Receiving a letter like this will make her so sad and grief-stricken, but the two of us must sacrifice ourselves in order to save many others.

February 15, 1945 Cloudy

A huge enemy force has appeared off the coast of Japan, which means that the probability for a large-scale air attack is extremely high. We had, therefore, to rerun drills for the removal or at least the scattering of such important items as clothing. Consequently, the overnight stay which I had looked forward to was cancelled, and we were kept busy running around all day long. —Once the enemy force has been sighted, it is hard to see how the whole war situation could possibly have become more critical.

Lately even the very term "*hijōji* (an emergency/crisis)" has gone out of use. Although the word was commonly and frequently used in days gone by, the sense of emergency which prevailed then—and which *hijōji* connotates—is entirely different from our current situation. But indeed when things are as tense as they are, why do we remain idle?

There are plenty of flyers, but there are no planes to fly. When one looks back at the war in its entirety, the power of sheer material strength is obvious. In the long run, I would judge that *the* factor which enables a country to win the final victory has little to do with spirit or morale—it is rather the overwhelming quantity of its material goods.

It seems that Ms. K is getting married, so I am feeling a little lonesome. There is only one complete solution to all the vastly complicated problems surrounding such a business: marriage. Perhaps under these particular circumstances it is indeed the best solution. Most probably she will be wed without saying anything to or about me and I do not plan to say anything either—not even a word of congratulation. I do not wish to bring the ideal relationship between us down to the level of reality merely by mouthing words. If all this were only a dream dreamt in the springtime of my life, then it would be fine as a dream; it would be a lot better than an ugly reality. Still, the feeling of letdown refuses to go away. I will remain behind the scenes, but shall pray for her happiness.

March 1, 1945   Clear, with occasional clouds

At ten in the morning and in a grand auditorium, our commandant named the members of the First Kitaura Special Attack Unit which of course included myself. At this point there is no need for me to write about how ready I feel (to face a certain death).

For a long time now I have been emotionally prepared for this, and I only pray that the day will come soon. Sometimes with only resignation—and sometimes bravely—until today I have only been marking time. Just momentarily, when my name was called by the Commandant, my mother's face appeared before me and then vanished.

Dear Father, Mother, and younger brother and sister, I wish you happiness.

April 12, 1945

The final decisive battles between ourselves and the enemy on and around the main island of Okinawa have finally become so critically important that Japan's very survival is at stake. Sinking as many enemy ships as possible is right now of the utmost urgency, and our seaplane unit has finally been designated for a special attack. There was a naming ceremony at seven in the morning for the members of the Special Attack Unit, following which, in the afternoon, its first group bravely took off to join in the battle. The rest of us sent them off with heartfelt *bō-fure* (waving of hats).

Of course, I too am a member of the Special Attack Force; regrettably, I was not chosen for the first group, but I will certainly be among the next to leave for the battle. Taking into consideration the time and days required for preparation of the aircraft, most probably I shall be able to leave in five or six days—the sooner the better, even by a day. My heart is as calm as still water and as bright as a mirror. There is nothing at all to worry about back home, but I wish I could see my parents' faces just once more before I leave. Even though it is impossible, I wish I could go after having talked with them to my heart's content. I wish that I at least had their pictures. . . .

I was not a particularly good son, and I took it for granted that I could certainly have a vacation once I finished the course of my schooling. So long as I had the vacation, I thought that I could get together with my parents anytime; that was my first and fundamental mistake, but I am going to compensate for this *oya-fukō* (failure to live up to filial piety) of mine by my striking (the enemy) with my own body.

Since there is not much time left before I leave, I decided as of today to wrap up this diary of mine. For nearly a year now I have been describing my student life here at Kitaura, though of course there have been certain omissions.

To convey the emotional truth of the time from which I was first named as a member of a Special Attack Force and then trained to hit the enemy with my own body, is not something that one can set down with a pen. The state of mind involved here is something which only those with the same experience can feel and understand, and so I would not even attempt to write about it.

Goodbye Father, Mother, Younger Brother, and Younger Sister—
and all my teachers/mentors/professors as well.

I pray for your good health.

GAIKAKU, Yasuhiko

> Born June 19, 1922.Through Shizuoka Higher School, entered the
> University, Faculty of Economics, April 1942. Entered the Navy
> Corps, December 1943. Killed in action near Okinawa, April 14,
> 1945.

—His will, addressed to his mother, written at the time of his departure as a member of the Kaiten Special Attack Corps—

Dear Mother:

Please forgive me for not having written you over such a long
time.

Mother, although I suppose I should begin with the conventional
"I trust that you are as well as usual," I can very well imagine the many
hardships you must be undergoing nowadays. The reason for my pick-
ing up a pen today is to write something which I hope will be considered my will. As you know, I am such a touchy soul to begin with that
I find it rather unacceptable for someone like myself, who am so full
of life, to be forced to think about death and what comes after it and to
feel tragic about himself. I have personally meant to leave nothing
behind, and neither do I need to leave any instructions for you about
how to handle my affairs in the event of my death.

So if, more or less, all this amounts to is just another letter, there
is really no excuse for my having neglected writing for so long. This is
especially the case for someone who, when I was home, used to talk
with you tirelessly until two or three o'clock in the morning. I thought
that now would be a good time to renew those chats, and so I should
like to write to you little by little, as the thoughts come to my mind.

This preface has gotten a little out of hand, but . . . .

1. How much I changed while I was away from your side, Mother.

While I was a student, I felt rather cold about everything. The only
things that I could get excited about were reading books and sports.
Occasionally I developed other interests, and one of them was theater:
Jōruri (Japanese traditional ballad drama). Another would be what I

might call the history of manners and customs, which are actually old folk tales with some romantic and sexy elements in them—and that was just about it.

Even after I entered the military there has been no significant change in my basic emotionalism. I am still the same lazy—but good-natured—person. Perhaps the only thing that has altered is the much greater strength of my past tendency to be fussy about trivial, everyday matters—like an old man. In other words, I have become very small-minded about a lot of things. I think that this happened because of my complete disgust with and disappointment in professional military men; they totally fell short of whatever limited expectations I had entertained about them.

They (the professional military men) are completely preoccupied with formality, and they deal with us and order us about formalistically both because that is Naval tradition and because it is in line with their personal normative standards as well. Yet the fact is that their *modus operandi* is nothing more than an obstinate convention which small-minded, insular people have steadily built up. Moreover, we both think that the convention could not be less important and that, precisely because we do think that way, we should just shrug it off when they accuse and criticize us. This would be especially true for someone like myself, who never had an ounce of competitive spirit in his whole life. If it were peacetime I would pay no attention at all and consider the whole thing irrelevant. But ever since I came into the military life my sense of opposition has somehow and strangely become much stronger. As a result, I have been conducting myself with a single aim in mind: to avoid giving them any opportunity to put me down.

What I am actually doing is taking special care not to have them nail me for doing something that is supposedly wrong but which, in the past, I would always have considered merely trivial and insignificant. It is no more than natural, then, that I have developed into a rather nervous person. Deep inside, however, I have always had the utmost disdain and contempt for the so-called military spirit; therefore the more they tell me to get rid of the *shaba-ke* (the civilian's attitude—i.e., worldly desires and ambitions) the closer I cling to it. I think that if I lost that there would be nothing left to be proud of, and that if others saw me living a life without it they would consider it a life filled with hypocrisy, extreme small-mindedness and even cowardice. At any rate, it is a simple fact that, out of having to live this life for over a year now, I have developed the kind of inner strength which enables me to say "go to hell!" and to laugh mockingly to myself regardless of what was done to me—*and* to continue to be obstinate. (Of course I understand that, under similar circumstances, the professional Navy men would manage to put a smile on their faces while crying inside their hearts.)

In any case, all these things now belong to the past, and I can no longer concern myself with them. Perhaps it would be more accurate to say that, with the exception of what I consider to be my personal duties, I have become totally unconcerned about everything.

2. About death.

From the time I entered the military I kept saying that I was not afraid to die. Even though I believed what I said, I was really talking like a fool. The very fact, however, that over and over again I had to keep saying so loudly and so aggressively that, after all, the loss of life was nothing to cry about, itself signified to me that I *did* have a very strong concern over matters of "life and death." The truth was that, even as I was saying that I had transcended these matters, until very recently the subjects had never really left my mind.

Perhaps it was because of the type of work I do that I could not help thinking the way I was at the time. I knew what I would eventually have to do, but had not as yet had any formal training for how to do it. It was just about that time (the last three months of last year), when I was in that frame of mind, that I used to agonize over a whole range of questions:

"How can we make our lives valuable?"

"For whom are we sacrificing our lives?"

"Wouldn't it be a useless death?"

"I don't want to die in this manner or that," etc.

Once our training began, however, I completely stopped thinking about death, and any need I felt to think about such matters no longer existed—it all simply disappeared from my mind.

Now I matter-of-factly carry out the job that I have to do without considering it a moral proposition—i.e., either as something we should do or something as heavy as the so-called military man's professional responsibility. I prefer to look at it as a "job" in the most lighthearted sense of the term, something like deciding whether or not it is time to go to bed. Right now my views of life and death are strictly on that level. It may not be an entirely suitable way of expressing these concepts, but my current mindset dictates that I should accept things as they are and live life the best way I can. Once that is accomplished, both life and death—and everything else—will go just fine.

Because I managed to devote an entire page of a large-size college notebook to the subject, while at the same time claiming that I had transcended the whole matter of life and death, I fear that I may have left myself open to a challenge: "On the contrary, does not your long note constitute evidence that you still have a strong concern about death?" —Any answer, however, would have to be in the negative.

I am happy about the fact that, because of the very nature of my job, the details surrounding my death—when and where and under what circumstances it occurs, etc.—will never ever be told to my family. I wrote the note simply because there was an off-chance that you might wonder and worry about just what my state of mind was when I died. I wanted you to know how very much I enjoyed my life until its final moment and that, with a peaceful heart, I am simply going to disappear from this world just as a light goes off.

Finally, I apologize for causing you so many worries by having been so selfish and doing *katte na koto* (whatever I wanted to do). Be that as it may, however, I think that on the score of filial piety I was a fairly good son.

All joking aside, if circumstances permit and you have the opportunity, please visit my old "battle-ground" (the place where I studied so hard) in Shizuoka, and remember the old days. Those were the days of my life when I was so enthusiastic and in such high spirits, and it remains the most unforgettable time for me. I even think that, should I ever come back as a ghost, I would like to be the way I was then.

The time for my departure is fast approaching, so I had better excuse myself. Please, everyone, stay well.

Written on the morning of a mission.

Yasuhiko

I am about to leave for a sortie, and my heart feels somehow purified or ennobled—like the clear color of lapis lazuli (sky blue).

NISHIMURA, Hidehachi

> Born November 12, 1916. Entered the University, Faculty of
> Economics, from Mito Higher School, April 1939. Conscripted
> August 1941. Died of an illness contracted on the battlefield, some
> twenty kilometers northwest of the Mountain State of Luzon
> Island, June 25, 1945.

(From Chinchou, China. —Received September 5, 1941)

August 15, 1941—Departed from Takasaki.

I wondered how I would be able to walk in full gear and with such a heavy knapsack. My uniform reminded me of the chill of our school uniforms, so somehow things did not feel just right. I absent-mindedly walked along a back street for about half a ri (1 *ri* = 2.44 miles), just tagging along at the end of a line. Shortly afterward we took a little break in the yard of a primary school. For security reasons, the whole trip was conducted under heavy guard. The great weight on my shoulders, which are not used to carrying heavy things, increased at an accelerated rate. It was a cloudy day and here and there I caught glimpses of puddles. Finally, and shortly after noon on that hot, midsummer day, we formed a line and quietly walked up the steps to the freight-train platform of the Takasaki station. Complete silence. Each person is wide-eyed and quiet, not exactly a surprise in light of the fact that our fate was turning so mysteriously. Everything around was painted in a camouflage which was somehow alarming.

After waiting for the command we boarded the train in an orderly line, and again in silence. The windows on one side were all tightly shuttered. Not a soul had been sent to see us off, and there was no sound of anyone shouting "*Banzai!*" (as was usually the case when soldiers were being sent off for the front line) when the train left the platform to the dull sound of its own wheels. Shortly after departure, train lunch boxes for two meals and a bag of candy were handed down to each of us. I looked out the window aimlessly and, lacking the ability to feel, took mental stock of myself. I looked at the bed, then at the ceiling, sucking on candy the whole time. Except for a stop to change tracks at Ōmiya, our train ran at full speed straight to Tokyo.

(From southern China—Received December 22, 1941)

A third-day moon (crescent moon) with part of its light stolen by black clouds is throwing itself onto the ridges of mountains that are edged in black. There are two villages at the bottom of our ridge and they cast dark shadows. As soon as the sun goes down it is as though these villages change into black souls, and on many nights we strain our eyes for a clue to this strange puzzle. —In the mountain villages in this area, where there is no electricity, the flickering rushlights of lamp wicks go on and off beyond the watery fields. The people who live here are apprehensive that these lights might leak; nonetheless they occasionally come on, and on this point we become simultaneously suspicious and irritated.

Once the moon disappears, the land in front of us suddenly turns into complete darkness. Of course as one concentrates on finding a light, one's eyes become accustomed to the darkness. It was at just such a moment, almost as if *omoiawaseta yōni* (with a montage effect), a beautiful glitter of stars typical of the southern skies emerged from a thin veil of other stars in a deep blue sky. This is when the deep and clear continental skies unfold their greatest beauty, and when each of the constellations, at different distances, clearly insists on its own space. Those stars nearest us look softly light, and those farther away look cold even in this place where summer never dies. As I look at the busy group of stars I remember the beautiful lights of cities.

My personal yearning, however, somehow seems to be something like a dream that floats along on a separate orbit, just like those of the endless stars. Even though this world looks up at the same stars, the rows of houses which are bathed in their light are here and there in ruin —not more than a ghastly jumble of mud and bricks. I objectively took note of myself too—standing alone on a hill in blank surprise, and even, for once, forgetting about my nostalgia for home.

(From Kuangtung Hospital, southern China—Received on August 13, 1942)

When I said that I had absolutely no need of any star (on my shoulder, i.e., designating a higher rank), old man Miyagi challenged my statement: "You may easily say such a thing, but there is really no one who, at heart, does not wish for advancement." —So I decided to set him straight, and said:

"I am absolutely indifferent concerning this matter of getting or not getting a star. A similar situation would arise should you not particularly feel like eating *o-shiruko* (a traditional Japanese sweet soup made of red beans). Do you not think that it would be less of a bother simply to skip the *o-shiruko* and instead to stay home and perhaps take a nap? Or would you prefer to walk a long distance carrying a canteen, and then have to wait in line for a long time in order to buy it? Even in the same sort of situation, however, if someone else was kind enough to purchase the *o-shiruko*, brought it to me, and asked me to drink it, then I would be happy do so.

Stars are something I simply cannot care less about, exactly like the *o-shiruko* when I do not care to have it. Neither do I wish to earn one by lowering myself and working hard obsequiously. Just being a private first-class is enough for me. Promotions will not make me happy, and I would not become overly excited even if my pay went up by a yen or two. If they actually offered to give me a raise, however, that would not be a problem and I would gladly take it.

I only respect a man of character, perhaps because, intellectually, I am conceited enough to believe that I can match any officer's intelligence. Basically, when I hear noncommissioned officers giving their views on rank, and other officers boasting about their intellectual superiority, I cannot help but feel that such behavior only amounts to some sort of shallow illusion—that it is completely without substance, in fact, a great many people completely misunderstand the distinction between the nation's right to rule and every individual within that nation's exercising his or her individual rights. Perhaps my notions are not easy to understand, but my statement about not wanting to be promoted is based on a certain special kind of self-confidence."

(An uncensored letter from New Guinea which he had a staff officer who was returning to mainland Japan bring back for him. — Received on September 18, 1943)

On August 23rd I received both the letter posted on June 29th and a few journals: *Kaizō* (*Reform*), *Current of the World*, and *Tanka Kenkyū* (*Tanka Poem Study*). I am able to use the glasses by tying a string to the rim. I can manage all right since I was able to borrow both a dictionary and a miniature dictionary.

My assignment nowadays is not as a signal corpsman (or telegraphist) or even anything close to that. I am an interpreter for Division Headquarters and am also connected to the Information Office. I have already been an interpreter for half a year, and on three different occasions I participated in the interrogation of Australian flyers. Aside from that, my major tasks involve translating captured documents and maps. I have become quite comfortable in speaking the indigenous people's language, but I am not nearly so good at breaking down the enemy's radio communication.

As for my everyday life, hiding in a virgin forest which is no more than a muddy jungle is not very pleasant. We are allowed to cook only in the evening and, surrounded as we are by "morasses of mud," our two meals are simply awful. You should know that our location is near Salamaua, New Guinea. Despite this, however, you should be relieved to know that I regard my work here at Headquarters as my good fortune and believe that I shall survive so long as Headquarters itself is not destroyed.

The horrors of the fighting on the Salamaua front are comparable to those of Attu Island and Guadalcanal. I wish I could persuade myself that Japanese soldiers are the toughest in the world, and that they do not need to be worried about by the people back home. For the future I would like to see as many Japanese youths as possible grow up into the kind of men who would consider the offering up of their own personal lives as an honorable thing to do. Salamaua has been under attack and taken an average of a hundred bombs a day, and for as long as fifty days in succession; all houses were completely destroyed, and even the shape of mountains has been changed.

There are several thousand huge bomb craters all over the place, and in one spot a second bomb as large as five hundred kilograms was dropped directly on top of another, original crater and enlarged the original to a depth of about eight to ten meters and a diameter of over twenty meters. About five dozen planes are constantly pressing us from the skies, a mixture of four-engined consolidated B-24s, Boeing B-17Es, twin-engined North American B-25s, and others. Regrettably, the enemy right now has complete command of the air here in New Guinea. So it is that I too have suffered the misfortune of drifting for some three hours on Dampier Strait. The road from New Britain to New Guinea was perhaps a *Shingun-fu* (lit., a funeral-march music) from heaven to hell. Still, our Japanese troops are fighting as best they can even though surrounded by foes on all sides.

I would say that our bitter fighting on the Salamaua front is currently the worst campaign of the war that Japan is fighting. The Shigeki Platoon Leader and also the Terayama Company Commander have been killed in action, as have my friends Shōzō Nakajima, Lance Corporal Shiraishi, whom you met in Takasaki when you came to visit me, and Second-Class Private Shigeki too. All perished in the Dampier Strait.

I am unquestionably a very lucky man, and now that I have arrived at Headquarters, dear Father and Mother, it is all right for you to feel fully relieved. Of course I am more than prepared to offer my body in meeting an honorable death but, reduced as we now are to only a fifth of our original number, it seems somehow that we are miraculous survivors. —Mr. Tokuhei Ojima said that he too had drifted in the sea for three days: I wonder what is happening to him now on the front line.

The fact is that the situation is extremely grave, and that thousands of enemy shells come flying our way every day. And if the ordinary people back home ever experience the type of air raids that we are experiencing now, they will be screaming in agony and even become so terrified that they will lose their minds. More than a few times bombs have fallen within sixty feet of me, but I remain undisturbed and even take a nap, stretching out with an air of perfect composure. —I am not terrified and feel no discomfort. With my fingers in my ears because otherwise a bomb blast would break my eardrums, I am in an air-raid shelter listening to the bombing. Occasionally a strong wind rises up to blow in our direction, briefly steals the heat away and then quickly passes on.

If I wrote too much more I would have nothing to talk about when I come home, so I shall stop writing here and now. The fighting here in New Guinea is desperate and deadly, but I still feel certain that I will be able to come home by next spring. Right now I am in very good health and full of energy. Since a staff officer here is returning to mainland Japan, he will be kind enough to mail this communication from there.

August 26   Written in Lolo

HACHIYA, Hiroshi

Born March 18, 1922. From the Sixth Higher School, entered the University, Faculty of Letters, Japanese Literature Department, April 1943. Entered the barracks in December, 1943. Sent to Iwō Jima, December 1944.

—Diary—

(During the time of Army Air Engineering School)

There is the sound of an engine, and
an azalea looks lonely.

The infirmary is *nigoru* (muddy, not clear)
    because of the fatigue from official inspections.

I dreamt of my beloved plane that did not return,
    and a summer field is on fire.

Having seen off a wartime friend, I am alone in a barracks
    and writing a travel diary.

Along with an air-raid warning, preparations are being made
    against the onrush of *tsuyu* (the rainy season).

October 1944

It is a rainy day again today, and this marks three days of intermittent rain, for a simple soul like myself perhaps this is very timely luck. Still, it is awful for me to try and feel that this situation in which we find ourselves—a cloudy airport and a plane sitting sadly in the rain—should be any cause for rejoicing. I am, however, almost getting used to the style of life here; or I should rather say that I have been made to become used to it. There are many unpleasant things, but there are some pleasant ones too. The time between dinner and roll call is when my heart finds the most peace. This is the time I use to reflect upon myself, to reminisce about things back home, or to recollect my mother's words. My hometown is my biggest treasure and, because it exists, I am alive. All I really want is to live a free life and be able to read a book at my mother's side. Such things are not permitted in the military, however, and each individual's thoughts are extremely restricted. Things that seem completely nonsensical and foolish outside of military life are considered perfectly normal within it.

I heard that a typhoon is due to arrive tonight, so perhaps tomorrow will be another rainy day. Beginning today, I will be assigned to act as student duty officer for the week. There is no responsibility involved, but I am hoping that I can get through the week without making a mistake. I have recently been praying much less to gods and divine spirits, and I am certainly lacking in respect for them. I know that this is not a good situation and that I should change it, but I have just become lazy about the whole thing. Perhaps to a certain extent I am leaving matters to fate. But if I think a little more deeply, I realize this is no good. I am a human being who has always lived in complete submission to the great will of the divinity, and will live that way from here on in. It is obvious and I know for sure that, when I forget to do this, the end will come. I think I need to pray much, much more.

The life here is really an interesting one. When it rains, we do not have anything to do.

—From his memo of the Battle of Iwō Jima—
(The following poems are tanka)

Iwō Jima is so tranquil in the smoky-gray rain;
    yesterday's cannonade must have been a dream.

(December 9, 1944)

I am writing a poem in a bomb-shelter and
    listening to the sound of the bombs;
    How pitiful it is that the springtime of my life is now about to
    end.

(December 13, 1944)

Struggling through the loneliness of this southern land,
    I am alive in a bomb-shelter filled with the breath of others.

How pitiful is a man who has to live so alone, in a bomb-shelter
    that is becoming ever more foul from the comrades' breath!

(December 14, 1944)

We glare angrily at a darkening cloud over Iwō Jima:
    The sun has gone down as we wait for a plane that has not yet
    returned.

(December 17, 1944)

NAGASAKA, Shin

> Born October 3, 1923. Through the Urawa Higher School, entered the University, Faculty of Economics, October 1943. Entered the barracks, December 1943. Killed in action August 14, 1945, 4 o'clock in the afternoon at a point between Mutankiang and Murin in Manchuria.

(A postcard to his Mother—April 1945, in Manchuria)

How have you been, Mother? Naturally I am concerned about our capital city Tokyo because I am uninformed about what is happening there. Here it seems as though winter is reluctant to leave us. I have been a bit *heikō* (annoyed by, beaten, dumbfounded) lately by reason of the dismal life we lead here, even though it is a situation over which I have no control. As a result, trivial and unimportant things go through my mind. Unlike during the whole course of my student days—except of course for outward appearances—my present situation deadens such feelings as self-reproach and impatience in favor of the feeling that I am adequately performing my duties. Lately this escapism and complacency is becoming offensive and annoying, and I rather despise myself. It is as if something heavy is hanging over me, and I feel that the need to somehow get out of this is something I should pay immediate attention to.

Incidentally, please let me know Daiden's (a male cousin) full name and his address in Yamaguchi.

(A letter addressed to father and mother, June 1945—the last letter, from Manchuria)

My Dear Father and Mother:

Lately it has been raining softly every day, very much like the *tsuyu* (rainy season) in mainland Japan. I have heard that the weather this year is expected to be more irregular than usual. It is June already, and yet it is so cold that I still feel the need to use the heater now and then. I spent everyday looking up at the skies and mudding my long rubber boots. Anyway, how has everything been with you lately? I get so worried when I think about our house in Tokyo. Everyone I run into these days asks me the same question: "Is your house still there?" Of course what they want to know is whether or not our home has been bombed or destroyed yet. This has become a standard greeting nowadays. —If possible, please move away from Tokyo soon.

It has already been five months since my arrival, and before I knew it I had already become a senior *minarai* (officer cadet class). The life here is not what most civilians would think it is. In my interaction with others, and officers, I have often become totally disenchanted. On each of these occasions, I kept urging myself to compensate for my weakness and to go on doing my duty. I do not concern myself with how tough things get so long as they have to do with my fundamental duties, but I do not like to waste my energies by paying attention to certain unnecessary matters.

I wonder whether or not the world is supposed to be like this. Inexperienced as I am in the ways of the world, perhaps it may be that things which seem so unreasonable to me are in reality normal and reasonable. Still, I do not believe that our normal *modus operandi* is a good way to live. The only people with whom I feel in perfect accord are my colleagues in the true sense of the term, (i.e., the university students who were mobilized into the military). When I think about these things I feel very nostalgic about my boyhood. How happy I would be if I could only return to those past but genuinely pure ways of thinking (of innocence and sincere good will)! I also recall my innocent playmates of those days and wonder how and where they are now.

I have had a picture taken with Cadet Miyakoshi which I shall be sending you later.

Well, then, please take good care of yourselves, and especially in such times as these. I will be *ganbari-masu* (do my best, stand out stoutly) i.e., doing my best, in good health.

Respectfully,

Shin

SUGIMURA, Yutaka

> Born February 6, 1923. From the Tokyo Higher School, entered the University, Faculty of Jurisprudence, April 1842. Entered the Naval Training Corps, December 1943. Killed during training at Chitose Air Base, Hokkaidō, July 1945.

—Diary—

June 11, 1945

I read the late Sasaki (Hachiro Sasaki)'s posthumously published writing, "Miyazawa Kenji: *Ai to Ikusa to Shi ni Kanren-shite* (Miyazawa Kenji: On Love, War and Death)," (See pp. 1–5), and I was very deeply touched. I really regret that I did not have the opportunity to carry on a serious conversation with him, and all my memories are about our arguments and quarrels over things quite trivial. Just as what I used to say that "those grown-ups who enjoy reading children's stories are great": he went to his death exactly like that, demonstrating the fact that he possessed a great soul. ....

June 24, 1945

Raining since this morning. It is soft and calm, and a very pleasant day. I wrote letters to friends S and N, and completed reading the middle volume of a book—*Gēte to no Taiwa* (*A Conversation with Goethe*). In doing so I touched the world that I had been away from for quite some time and also something powerful and strong: *Productivitä* (productivity), *Aktivität* (activity), and *Geistesleben* (intellectual life). A man can overcome anything with his faith and a vigorous courage to help him, but he can just as easily be immediately destroyed while under a cloud of suspicion.

Hate does not hurt people: what destroys people is contempt.

So far as Byron is concerned, we should not cherish only those who are pure or moral. If we recognize everything great—that recognition makes us culturally enriched.

My Higher School period: where and when so many things happened (to me): we grew angry together, laughed together, shared both joys and tears, and we got so upset about so many trivial things in those days—but it was the most memorable period of my life.

Dear Mr. Kameo, I think that the foundation of my ideology was laid down both by yourself and by the German language. It was also during that period that I opened my eyes to see the human world for the first time.

June 29, 1945

I am writing this on a train heading for Ueno after having finally parted from my mother, Tae, and Shizu. At this point I hardly think that I will ever see them again in this world. I parted from them by sticking my neck out of a window of the train and waving my hands until I could see them no more. At the station my mother gave me some advice: "Before you leave, talk with your father about anything and everything. You may not want to tell me some things because you think I would cry if you opened up to me." —Her words touched my heart deeply, but it is better to part just like that—softly and gently.

Mother had also said something earlier which made me a little angry: "Someone asked me to ask you whether or not those who join the Special Attack Forces really do so as gladly as is reported in the newspapers." For my part at least, I shall indeed go gladly both because I think it is for the good of the country and because I consider it my duty as a Japanese.

So far as more detailed revelations about what is in my heart, I intend to set it all down at a much later date.

Good-bye, Mother and Taeko.
Good-bye, the Sea of Japan.
Your son, your elder brother, and your friend is now leaving for
     war with a high heart.

As I pray for the prosperity of the nation,
I think ahead to the world where we will meet each other again.
—Good-bye, farewell, and please stay well.

After departure,
I sit alone by the window
on a train trip.
Over the hill where evening primroses (*oenothera tetraptera*)
     bloom,
Ocean, forests, and pine woods,
—I continued to look back even as the train moved forward.
It was such a sad train trip.
Such a sad train trip, all alone.

June 30, 1945   (Written on the train from Karuizawa to Ueno)
     When I stepped off the train at 1:30 in Karuizawa I had already been standing ever since Naoezu.
     I wandered around in the rain for a while, trying to decide whether or not to go to Ms. S's place. It was not as cold as I had anticipated. There were so many people in the waiting room that I simply went to a corner near a restroom and sat down. I wanted to sleep but could not. At 2:30 I ate a box lunch; at 5 [*sic.* an error for 3?] I went to rent a bicycle, gathered my luggage together back at the station, and got ready to leave. —Suddenly Ms. S and Ms. I appeared and called out to me, I was startled.
     I just stood there with my mouth open. I told myself that perhaps, since I had at least seen them once again, I should not go so far as to visit their home. But of course I did accompany them to their home, simply because it was *oshii* (too precious an opportunity to miss out on). I strolled alongside of my bicycle while Ms. S and Ms. I, using a single umbrella under a gentle rain, walked together on a tree-lined road and discussed just about everything. They told me that they came

today to buy tickets for Takasaki in order to see me off. Little Ms. H had come to the station yesterday and copied the train schedule; then they all put their heads together to try and pinpoint which train I might be on. When Ms. T said that I would have to be on the 1:30 train and that she was going to the station no matter what, certain other family members disagreed, said it was impossible, and were opposed to her coming.

The night before, after Ms. T returned from Tokyo, no one had an appetite, but everyone agreed that this was just as well because it would save rice. The mother of the family was crying especially hard. It was decided that a fine would be levied if anyone mentioned me, but as it turned out they were all about to be bankrupted: they said that there was still talk of me despite the threat of a fine.

I put the best possible interpretation on this story and felt very grateful, truly sensing the genuine good will of the S family.

As for Ms. S herself, she told me that it would have been better had I not come. She said that I was cruel and then went on: "If we had just played tennis and left it at that, I would never have had to experience such a tragic situation." Perhaps that may be true, and I may be the type of man who only spreads sadness wherever he goes.

There was nothing more in particular to talk about, and lingering there for who knew how many more hours would not solve anything. Still, time simply ran on too fast. I had changed the original 7:06 [sic.] departure time to 6:22, and started to walk towards the station. Halfway there, I found myself under an umbrella with Ms. S, and we walked the tree-lined road. I was so happy. I was also so resentful about time's quick passage and the increasing nearness of the station.

I saw the mountains with rain clouds hanging heavily over them, as well as the white houses of Akakawane and the long stretch of the tree-lined road; I felt a drizzling rain, and my oneness of existence with the girl beside me.

I had to fight so hard against my desire to kiss her and to hold her tight. At this writing, I still regret very much that I did not follow the voice of my heart and conducted myself accordingly.

I cannot understand why or to whom I intended to expose myself by writing something like this. I suppose that this is simply a side of me that I was not familiar with.

—On a train, and reflecting on my psychological state in connection
with joining the Special Attack Force—

My life's goal has been to live every day as the best human being
I could possibly be. More specifically, I wanted to live as the best
Japanese I could possibly be and I always considered any effort
expanded to move myself closer to that ideal as just about the noblest
thing I could do. I found a value in that effort itself. I simply wish to
live as a truly first-rate Japanese. In the final analysis, that is all. You
could say it is a shame that I spent twenty-three years in studies before
entering the military. I am convinced, however, that studying is not an
end in itself; the ultimate value is to be found rather in a process within which studying is only one element—and so I am content. As a matter of fact I believe that, at least in the context of ultimates, my past
studies were not a waste at all. I probably did not study enough! At any
rate, I certainly cannot shut out the feeling that I would like to live a
little longer, and there are probably a couple of reasons for this:

1. In the first place, the desire to live is implanted in the nature of
any living being, no matter how hard or how painful that life might be.

2. A second reason would be the presentiment that, if I did manage to survive a bit longer, some good things just might be in the off-
ing. Then, of course there is the awareness of what an absurd irony it
would be if, by some remote chance, I should turn out to be one of the
last casualties in this war.

—Of course all of these things are left far behind when compared
to what is required of us by our primary ideology.

July 5, 1945

I arrived at my post in Chitose today. I have great expectations,
and apparently everyone has been assigned to a specific group. —
Starting tomorrow, flight training will begin at last.

INOUE, Hisashi

> Born May 1, 1922. Entered the University, Faculty of Jurispru-
> dence, from Shizuoka Higher School in April 1942. Joined the
> Naval Training Corps in December 1943. Killed in action aboard
> the light cruiser Ōyodo on July 24, 1945.

—Song of a Hawk—

A hawk makes sorrowful cries in the great autumn skies,
    making circles and floating away.

—Thinking of someone while offering sacred *sake*—

The tears that fall on this sacred *sake*. . .
    Are not shed because my heart is in turmoil
        —but over thoughts of the wife of my heart.

—Purple Smoke—

Because life is so short,
    the dance of purple smoke is so sorrowful.

—A Nurse—

Pretending she hadn't noticed that flowers in a flower bowl were
    disarranged,
        a nurse came to check my pulse and left.

—Leaving the Hospital—

Wearing a military uniform this morning,
    which here lately has been
        such a rare experience,
            I actually feel new strength in my body.

My body which has been so afflicted and
    is now capable of praying
        for the well-being of those young military men who
            —as far as I could see—stood waving their hats.

There are also many nurses with whom I became acquainted
    standing in line—and making the loneliness of
        this morning's journey so overwhelming.

—Miscellaneous Poems—

Knowing so very well that there will be many negative things
   about my twenty-three years in this world
      —I dropped a fishing line.

However difficult and painful matters may present themselves as,
   I do not lose composure
      because I have been facing them down
         —and I do not have to say anything.

On an autumn day I climbed a hill and looked down upon
   sunlit chalkstone—I felt a certain sadness.

Sasanqua flowers —
   they would not hate anything even if
      I alone were to remain pure.

A sasanqua flower that single-mindedly and quietly
   Survives by seeping the cold water of a jar.

A sasanqua flower does not even talk openly of
   the quiet loneliness of autumn skies and earth.

I read a letter from my mother, to whom
   my life of twenty-three years
      cannot be substituted for
         by anything in this world.

SUMIYOSHI, Konokichi

Born February 15, 1921. From Shizuoka Higher School, entered
the University, Second Faculty of Engineering, Electric Engineering Department, in October 1942. Under the Student Mobilization
Act, worked at the Institute of Aeronautics Research, beginning at
the end of 1944. Killed by an air raid, May 24, 1945, together with
his entire family of seven when he returned home that evening, in
Meguro, Tokyo.

March 5, 1945   Cloudy

It has been a gloomy day, and I kept thinking deep thoughts about all sorts of things. I sat in front of a heater all day, and then came home early. Why do we have to say good-bye to those whom we love? I think too of the miserable condition of human lives these days, and of the tragedy involved in abusing nature's gifts to kill one another. However, one must be strong and tough. Regardless of how unpleasant things may become, an ultimate solution can only be reached through all-out efforts—and at every moment—on the part of every individual. I am confident that, out of love for my fatherland, I can face death in a serene frame of mind, but I cannot deny that I do have some questions about what is going on in this country.

The nation as a whole is not the problem, and indeed there is much about current Japan which may well be the answer. No one is more appreciative than I am of my good fortune in having been born in this beautiful land. But this same heart of mine that prays for our nation to become even more beautiful and sublime, also aches over a lack of conviction about too many things in today's Japan.

I want to do my best. I want to do whatever I really have to do with every ounce of my being. It would solve everything if I can do all this cheerfully and in high spirits.

March 7, 1945

Haircut this morning. Some say that any ideology which is not accompanied by action is worthless, and perhaps that is true. It might also be said that if an ideology were really thought through, the very expenditure of thought would itself be persuasive as to the value of practice. Still, I preferred to be rather casual in the practice of my own ideology, believing that, if one devoted all one's might to practice, everything would be over and done with much too soon. I planned that my own approach should be more natural.

Mental satisfaction might very well be achieved by doing one's best and by drowning in one's sense of fulfillment, but following this course results is nothing more than self-salvation. But I still mean to do my best, and believe that I would not give up even if I fell short. The easy life of compromise and taking thing as they come is not good, and neither is forgetting about the desire to live in the truth. Once again must I see myself as a solitary human being standing between this universe of ours and nation.

"And what is the nation?"

For me as well as for the nation, present conditions speak pretty much for themselves. But I cannot be satisfied with things as they are either for myself or the nation. My natural ambition, which could not be held down even if I tried to do so, seeks the true *sugata* (form the way it is) of me and of Japan. And so the current reality is by no means satisfactory. If we wish to discriminate between the positive and the negative elements of the world we live in, we need to elevate it to a higher and higher level. —In order to accomplish that, by far the most important thing we need is a strong and honest resolution.

I must endure a good deal of pain, because there is no way to find a solution except by enduring and suffering through and through. A true heart as well as hope will only begin to shine out through suffering and pain; and, therefore, I shall accept my current predicament. I must be duly thankful for whatever gifts I am already blessed with, and at the same time have to come up with even more fighting spirit. This is such a life as would destroy even my willingness to be a sacrificed stone, but that is only because I myself am still not strong enough. Even in —ko's case (reference to a girl the author had become friendly with while he was at the Aeronautics Institute)—and even in today's situation with its dark, unknown future—the two of us must share our true hearts and trust each other; we will have to go through sweat and tears to make this love of ours even deeper and truer. Yes, we will indeed make our love the truest and deepest possible; and that is why, dear —ko, I must ask you to endure today's suffering. I know how you must be suffering, but please put up with the pain for my sake. You must know how to pray, so please pray for us. And, with your tears, please purify our love even more. I shall labor even more mightily than before. As we watch our love develop into a truly great one, let us move on to the next stage in its creation—marriage.

What is certain is that, at this point, self-reflection should never be drowned in a foolish mood. Reality is too harsh. My body is being held to the fire (i.e., my life is in imminent danger). Notwithstanding all ideals and idealism, no matter how great, everything will be completely destroyed unless this fire is extinguished. Regardless of how uneventful and dry life might be, I should—if I relied on that ethical code of living which I have acquired over the past years—be able to live joyfully and with a sense of hope. Just now, however, that code does not seem quite good enough. The nation's tragic plight projects itself into part of the great, throbbing pain in my own heart.

Correspondingly, I also feel that the ethics of life I have learned may not be quite adequate to the situation. I would also think, however, that —even while suffering through this tragic passage in both our national and personal histories—the individual should be permitted to make his own best use of himself for the good of the nation, and to maintain his hope of feeling fulfilled in this life.

The two things that one must work at persistently are happiness and good health; from these spring cheerfulness and self-reliance.

March 20, 1945

Last night I immediately accepted the assignment for night duty. I was concerned about —ko's well-being, but I could not find her. I offered to assemble Ms. Karatsu's radio, but went to bed early—on Professor Inoue's bed—because of a bad headache. Mice were making so much noise at night! My phone call to —ko went through, and I finally returned home. My effort had been in vain. In the afternoon I asked Miyoko (a younger sister) to phone —ko for me and went to Yūtenji Station, but there was no luck there either.

Dear —ko, you might be listening. The music, the last program of today's broadcasting, is beautiful. —This evening, Miyoko informed me that —ko is going to *sokai* (move, evacuate from a city to a rural area for safety) to Nara. I just could not sit still, or even stand still; I placed a call to her home. I was told that she will be departing tomorrow, at Higashi Kitazawa Station at two o'clock. So, in the evening, I wrote a farewell letter which was composed along the following lines.

I do not have much time left, but until the end, the very end, I am going to maintain hope and continue to keep on trying. An endless hope bubbles up in me which is created by trust in this beautiful and righteous fatherland of ours, my own self-confidence—even though I may not be physically strong and am also weak-minded [note: this is no more than an idiomatic way of expressing modesty and unpretentiousness]—and especially my trust in —ko. My dear —ko, even though we will be separated by a very great distance, please stay well. You are a woman who always does her best at everything, but especially at prayer. I hope and pray that your sincerity, your striving and your prayers will be both the glory of and the support for those around you.

April 2, 1945

There are a hundred or perhaps two hundred days left in my life. I asked my father to please send my mother out of Tokyo, as well as other people who are important to us. —It is time for self-reflection. Do I have any real conviction? Whatever the case, I must truly treasure the short time that is left of my life. Now I am alone quietly. I am thinking about many things.

Convictions are so important. And I must have a determination to make the moment of my death as glorious as possible. I can feel simultaneously calm and very powerful about that. All the pain I went through in the past was not in vain. I do not fear death, but can only anticipate a beautiful end and my dying with a smile on my face. The reason is that I can devote myself totally both to the fatherland and to those I love. —But I will not throw my life away. There will not be many more times when I shall be able to walk up the stairs in this beloved two-story house or to look at the scenes which surrounded it. I must reflect more upon myself to check on whether or not I am living with the appropriate appreciation for each and every moment that remains to me. I shall devote myself to doing so.

My feeling now is that I can accept Buddha's teaching on this situation that "one must not meet those whom he or she loves." Dear —ko! I do miss her terribly and—without even the trace of a falsehood. I want to admit that I do. I want to see her. But even if I could it would be meaningless in the end. Life is certainly painful, and so fleeting. Having gone through it, at least to a certain extent, and reached the point of resignation, my emotion is calm simply because it is empty. —It is very calm indeed.

April 12, 1945

Last night I read a book on the theory of function until ten o'clock. Recently, and finally, I have reached *ochitsuite* (a psychologically settled and tranquil state of mind), and therefore I can read books with genuine interest. I got up at five o'clock this morning, and went to pick up a rear-car (a bicycle-drawn trailer). The resumption of an appetite is another pleasant side effect of this mood. Miyoko brought me *imomochi* (potato candies), and I want to share them with Ozawa and Ishii (two junior associates) when they come to visit. Despite of thinking this way, my appetite is still quite strong. If it were for —ko, and no matter what she might say, I would certainly have her eat it all. — I have been reflecting on things in general several times, and have decided that I must deal with everyone with the heart of a parent towards his own children.

April 13, 1945

Pulling a rear-car (a bicycle-drawn trailer), I went to the Aeronautics Institute. On my way there, I passed the front of the military barracks and became depressed—what a drab life military men lead! But I cannot be defeated by that sort of thing; I must be stronger. —And another premonition of mine came true: a letter arrived from —ko. A second letter came from Tsuchida (a classmate at Shizuoka Higher School). There are at least some things that turn hope into belief.

April 14, 1945

We suffered through a massive air-raid last night, so I went to work this morning somewhat later than usual. I did some unloading in the afternoon and then came home a little early. It was a spring day, and I feel rather sad. The cherry blossom season has already passed its peak. I watched a cadet training soldiers, shouting at them. All they are doing now is going through the motions, wasting time that is empty in the first place. It is impossible to find anything meaningful in meaninglessness. Eating, sleeping, giving false evidence of high spirits, and having to lie—that is the military.

April 15, 1945

Compulsory memorization of the Imperial Instruction for Soldiers has been imposed, and it is so foolish. This reaction reminds me that my feelings nowadays are gradually becoming more and more cosmopolitan. I find myself almost automatically locking into almost anything that falls outside Japan's traditional framework. I must build my own path more solidly, make the effort required and show the dauntless courage that I need in order to move towards that path.

April 26, 1945

A letter came from —ko. I feel uncomfortable about my own inability and my weak will. —ko is moving forward a step at a time. At this moment I feel that I have not quite come up to the mark, but at least I have the desire to be absolutely positive and *sunao* (gentle, honest, and open, i.e., the opposite of manipulative, rebellious, or pretentious). Moreover, and as I wrote in my "green notebook" (the small notebook that the author always carried with him), I am trying to be more appreciative, love people more, and make a real effort to practice that love assiduously. I am not quite up to that state of mind as yet, but I do believe that there is this path to take.

To die fighting in a war that we were winning would be easy. But, even given a situation wherein, in a losing effort, I were to be killed by enemy gunfire, I must still strive my very hardest to do my duty towards what I believe in and dream of.

April 30, 1945

I am totally discontented. I came home in silence, and with a depressed feeling so deep that I could not shake it off no matter how hard I tried. The skies were the clearest of blue. Such blue skies. From very early in the morning we were subjected to a large-scale raid. I went outside to sit on the lawn and (compose some poetry):

> It is so sad to have this helpless
>   feeling of pricking up one's ears for the
>   bombers' buzzing sound.
> I simply feel sorrow over
>   this bleak spring,
>   and think of someone far away.
> The springtime is passing away helplessly;
>   the sky is filled with light
>   and the wind is mild—
> Already full of the green leaves
>   that peak in this season.

This depression about not being able to fulfill my life, not only involves myself—inside and out—but other people as well, and indeed everything about the present situation. In short, everything is absolutely unpleasant. The tragic position that Japan finds herself in these days is the reason for all this, and there is no light at the end of the tunnel. —And I must part from my loved ones for that reason.

May 4, 1945

I keep writing over and over again, but never enough, about how simultaneously serene, tragic, and harsh this life is—and also about how I must become much stronger, more righteous, and more in command of the situation. My honest feeling about Japan is that I like it— rather, I love it. But instead of just talking about Japan's *kokutai* (national polity), and so on, I should think that the Japanese people ought to be thinking more broadly about the fate of all humankind. Mt. Fuji is so beautiful and serene, and if in fact love for the fatherland is the same thing as the love for one's hometown and his own people, then I feel that I have no less of it than anyone else. What I cannot understand or accept is the idea of fighting just for the past history and for the national polity. The emperor can do nothing to alleviate human-kind's miserable and tragic condition, unless every individual makes himself or herself better in order to accomplish that. Human beings must become much more broad-minded, and big-hearted too, and must know more about the sweat and tears of others. If this does not happen, then the fate of the human race will forever remain a tragic one. Truly, in order to rescue humanity from such a tragedy, we must all of us be most diligent both about choosing the best path to follow in our current situation, and about sticking to it after the choice is made.

May 6, 1945

We must create a new Japan from the ashes of the old. Because of those who speak so loudly of national policy, Japan has essentially penned itself up within a limited sphere and remained fearful of the outside world. Let us make the new Japan a place that is bright and full of hope. It should be vibrant with life and full of energy—like new green leaves when they sprout out. We cannot deny that we had high hopes for the old Japan. Of course, I do not intend to discuss such things as the longevity of the single Imperial bloodline and so on, but the fact is that the military totally ignored reality, as did those antiquated and stubborn so-called patriots, who trampled on the very nature of human beings and prevented our society from being developed in the way it should have been developed—and they did all this in the name of *kokutai*, the Imperial line, and the existence of the Imperial Prescripts. The simple fact in recent years was that these people controlled Japan and kept the Imperial glory from shining out. My wish would be to wipe out these feudal customs—such as separating members of the Imperial family from all commoners—that ignore basic human nature. What I would like to see is a society in which neighbors love one another and help one another, caring for the whole family of man and being genuinely grateful for all the good things in life.

May 16, 1945

Morning. I intended to spend the whole day reading. Yesterday we were assigned to do manual labor, and today I am spending a day this way. One thing, though: I felt an almost uncontainable joy in life welling-up inside me. I devoted every spare moment to reading the second volume of *Yoake-mae* (*Before the Dawn*) [by Tōson Shimazaki]. My thoughts immediately spring to a comparison between our national strength today and that of the past—and a quiet little hope also emerges. I really think I must make my own convictions much more firm. I also want to do my very best at cultivating myself in the direction of a broader vision with my utmost positive self-confidence.

I am in pain with longing for —ko. She is someone I can trust. I really believe that; still, I am quite anxious for a letter from her simply because there has not been a word for such a long time. As for thoughts about my parents and brothers and sisters—even as I was just walking down the street, my heart was simply hurting with my longing for them.

May 17, 1945

I carried Ms. Uno's luggage from Jomei-in Temple to Umishima Temple with Ms. Hirono, Mr. Yamada, and Mr. Yamanaka. The skies are eternally clear and high. Just as beautiful are those gigantic columns of clouds which keep rising up, and even the surface of the mountain can be picked out with great precision.

Everyone is in agony. I was very touched by *Doitsu Senbotsu Gakusei no Tegami* (*The Letters of the Fallen German Students*) [Japanese translation of selections from *Kriegsbiefe gefallener Studenten*, compiled by Philipp Witkop] as I read it for the second time. What a gap there is between idealism and the reality! And how painful is the suffering of those young men who give up their lives in war. My life too will last for just half of another year: there is no way to prevent that. I would be fooling myself were I to pretend that there could be space left in my heart for any little peaceful hope of salvation. Still, and although I am suffering and in pain, I want to continue to do my very best as long as I can. I continue to read *Yoake-mae* (*Before the Dawn*) by Tōson Shimazaki, and *Kumo to Kusahara* (*Clouds and a Grass Field*) by Kihachi Ozaki. It is a very quiet evening. I had some rice cookies that Ichi (a friend who had also been mobilized and worked together) offered me, and then I went outside. The light of the bow-shaped moon slanted down and shone faintly over the graveyard, and the starlit sky did not hold a single cloud. Singing the dormitory song—"Oh, Youth, skies, and life—this is the only life!" —I stepped on my own shadow, that had been made by the moonlight. For this last half a year, and for as long as they flow out like they are now, I shall never get bored writing about my deep feelings. Especially since those feelings are entirely free of pretense, I want to continue to write about them honestly—and I also wish to enter into an emotional state correspondent with them. Praising nature, enjoying life, and enduring the pain—my wish is that, each and every day, will afford me something to write down in this diary which I am planning to leave behind. Of course it is probable that the fires of war will consume the diary too. Regardless, I shall keep on writing anyway.

SUZUKI, Minoru

Born October 19, 1924. From the Eighth Higher School, entered the University, Faculty of Jurisprudence, October 1944. October 1944, entered the barracks. He suffered injury from the Atomic Bomb, on August 6, 1945, 8 a.m., and died at Ono Army Hospital, August 25, 1945, 9:30 p.m.

—Will—

August 25, 1945.   Nine o'clock in the evening
Dear Father and Mother:
    Please forgive me for having failed to fully live up to the duties of filial piety. Just when I was at last ready to be a good son to both of you and live up to my filial duties from now on, I have to fall short. I have always been most appreciative and grateful to you for your generosity in allowing me, despite our poor financial situation, to go on to the Eighth Higher School and from there to Tokyo Imperial University. I have caused you a lot of worry since my school days, and I am truly sorry and deeply regret that just now I have suffered such a serious injury—at that very point in my life when I was about ready to begin to make some returns on your kindness and all you have done for me.
    Both my older sister and younger sisters were considerate enough to put aside the idea of getting married, and instead they are helping you out and teaching grade-school children at the same time. I cannot find any words that would adequately express my gratitude to them.
    Father and Mother, you have always toiled so endlessly, getting up so very early in the morning with the moon still in the sky, and working away so steadily and hard until the stars twinkled at night—all in order to send me as far as the university. No appropriate apology is possible now. I am so sad that I am dying without returning all the kindness and everything else you did for me, while all I did was to cause so much hardship for you. However, my dear Father and Mother,

I am thinking that, even though my body dies, my spirit will always be in front of the *butsudan* (family Buddhist altar)—and it will be protecting you all, my beloved parents and sisters. When I become transformed into a spirit, I fully intend to serve all of you in filial piety. I will share laughter and sorrow together with all of you. Soon another autumn will arrive and you will hear hundreds of insects singing, and even when winter comes and the leaves are gone and the forest looks lonely—even then please do not cry. Regardless of whatever kind of situation you may be called upon to face, please take really good care of yourselves, deal with matters firmly and with conviction, and live on and on in good health.

Dear Father and Mother, the atomic bomb that was dropped the other day, on the 6th, was an extremely powerful one, and I suffered extremely severe burns on my face, back, and left arm. But I have received the kindest care possible under the hands of the attending Army doctors, nurses, and friends, and I feel very fortunate to die while being attended by the utmost care.

Minoru Suzuki

INAGAKI, Mitsuo

> Born March 12, 1924. From Tokyo Higher School, entered the University, Faculty of Jurisprudence, October, 1943. Entered the Navy Accounting School, October, 1944. Died at National Numazu Hospital, June 22, 1947.

(Translator's note: The following poems are all *haiku*, 5-7-5 syllables, and it requires a word or phrase indicating a season. The poems with the 5-7-5 format but without a season, and usually satiric, are called *senryū*.)

(From his *Haiku* notebook)

—Death—

The night has begun to extend itself,
  A lone star is in the sky.

No longer shall I be bitten
  by autumn mosquitos

—Coming Home—

A repatriated son, carrying a thought that
    has not been spoken—even to his late mother

At the tomb of my dear mother—her child has a doubt in his
    heart.
    And so his return is only a nominal thing.

In a dream dreamt in the chill of dawn,
    the longing for my departed mother was in vain

—Autumn Night—

My baby sister lives in the capital city, with a lone white star.
    It turned white on an autumn night while I was washing
    a bowl.

I eat a chestnut, and my thoughts of home
    grow even stronger.

The "X" of Gaffky[1] is sorrowful thing,
    In the darkness thrown by the young leaves outside the
    window.

—Twenty and three, a lonely autumn—

I shed tears in bed on a very cold night,
    pulling the spread over my head.

(Diary)

January 13, 1947 (Monday)   Clear
    10 o'clock in the evening.
    Mr. Nishijima's condition has worsened and he can no longer talk,
but his mind is quite clear. He is a man marked for death soon; indeed
its shadow has already enveloped him.

---

[1] Gaffky indicates the degree of advancement in a tubercular condition, and "x" under-
lines the extreme seriousness of such a condition.

The shadow of death too ought to be a happy one.

We should all share our happiness with one another, but that is so difficult to grasp.

Everyone has died away.

These are the only things I think about. Is it because I am superficial, or . . . ?

Midnight.

Mr. Ida bought me a flask with warmed *bōru-sui* (a liquid compound) in it for a hot water bottle. The other day he brought me a flask filled with a warmed chameleon solution. When I placed it on a heater, it became superbly beautiful as the red color of the heater brought out the red of the solution itself even more.

"Splendid!" "Splendid!"

Both Ida and Hirose were quite excited.

And today Ida brought me a *bōru* solution of a beautiful golden color. When I let my light shine on the flask, where all the lights were concentrated, it painted something like the shape of a sickle, like the tail of a comet. The kindness of a human heart! —This is not quite the same as the beauty of a human heart, or of human beauty itself, but it is extremely beautiful nonetheless, and when I touched the flask it presented something of a scientific beauty as well. When I became tired of looking at it, I put it inside my clothing (near my body as a warmer) again, and I studied while keeping my middle warm.

Additionally, I was given two—two!—delicious, pure white, and plump *daifuku* (sweet, traditional Japanese cakes).

May 12, 1947   (Monday)   Cloudy, then later gradually clearing

....

My sputum was examined today, and Gaffky has finally shown up. I am in absolute shock. After two years of medical care, I thought that I had finally seen the light at the end of the tunnel, and it is ironic indeed that just now Gaffky should be found for the first time.

When I think that perhaps I may have served as a means for the contamination of others, I half-consciously think that there is no way of apologizing to everyone. So far as my own emotions are concerned, although I cannot deny that there is a sense of tragic sadness, I feel that I should forget about it. All that I intend to do is to keep myself far away from everyone, on some mountain-top where there is no sign of people.

May 13, 1947

....

In the evening I could no longer stand the loneliness, so, with a mind full of memories, I went down to the river.

I was given a flower necklace from a child who was lying down on a carpet of flowers.—

—I am thinking that I will keep it in water and give it to Hirose.

When I returned to my room, I found that a beautiful large strawberry had been placed on my desk, and I wondered whose gift it was.

This beautiful strawberry is a great source of consolation for me.

—I realize that I have become very weak-hearted, and that I really reach out to the loving hearts of others.

My own heart has become softer too, and it feels lonely.

What I want is not necessarily a beautiful person,

or a large material fortune either.

What I long for is my love, of a healthy body, which I can devote to someone,

and a love of others that would not change regardless of time or situation.

May 17, 1947 (Saturday) Clear, and later gradually cloudy

The chief physician stopped by this morning to tell me that there is a cavity in the apex of my right lung. To say the very least, this is an extremely important matter. I was even able to face that terrible shock with relative calm (despite the fact that those two full years of medical treatment turned out to have been undergone completely in vain. Worse, those years turned out in fact to have been of a negative value.) Since I could not sleep last night, I kept thinking over all these things until deep into the night. At just about the time I was on the verge of falling asleep, I was thinking that I would not marry all my life, that I must resolve not to think of my own pain, and that I wanted to continue to live on for the sake of those who are even worse off than I am. Maybe it was that type of thinking that helped me to handle today's shocking news so surprisingly well. Anyway, my hope had been to return to the University, but that too has now become impossible. —In the morning, for a little while, I simply covered my cheeks in the white pillow and endured the sorrow.

May 18, 1947 (Sunday) Rain

It has been pouring rain since the middle of the night, and I don't think it will stop all day today.

—I think of her continually.

My love is so sorrowful.

For the first time, I sighed deeply and broke into tears.

Feeling utterly dejected,
      I let the raindrops put out my cigarette.   (a *haiku*)

May 26, 1947 (Monday) Cloudy

If possible, I plan to ask for surgery if there turns out to be a cavity at the highest point of my lung. I am already beginning to think along those lines.

At last, without telling her of my love, I returned again to the world of *roman* (fiction—the novel).

June 19, 1947

Surgery tomorrow. —Thoughts about my attachment to life and the immense amount of work that still awaits me.

I must conquer my illness for regaining an active life.

In this present state of confusion, I must find some order and put a certain rhythm into my life.

Once upon a time I felt such great pleasure in taking on the entrance examinations (for the higher school and also the University) simply because I was so confident of passing them successfully.

Energetic. Affirmation. Creation. (If only I could have them) I welcome pains.

POSTSCRIPT

The Humanity That Was Never Lost

—Committee for the Compilation of Writings
of the Students Killed in the War—

We are *ikinokotta* (i.e., we survived the war and are still alive). Throughout that harsh war, somehow we survived.

Why did we survive (i.e., why were we not killed like our friends)? For some of us it was simply because of our fate. Through the war experience, we came to realize seriously how awesome the power of fate is. There were some who were not killed just by chance. For example, I was strangely not hit by shrapnel from a bomb that exploded right near me, yet a *sen-yū* (my wartime friend) who was farther from the bomb was killed. Couldn't it be fate? Yes, it was fate. Even while fate smiled upon us (so that we survived the war), it was fate that attacked like a cold storm over our *gaku-yū* (fellow students, classmates) whose writings we are now reading posthumously. We, who had believed until then that history is something that moved steadily without any error even to the slightest degree, are made to realize how frightening fate can be for certain individuals.

Also there are some among us who survived by actively seeking survival. Aside from those who were already in the fields of natural science, who were automatically exempted from having to serve as soldiers, some took special measures to avoid conscription, e.g., by switching to medical school from the Belles Lettres track (humanities and social sciences) in a higher school, or some other way to avoid or delay getting drafted. They too had their reasons. They said that studying would contribute more to the welfare of the human race than going to the military. That was certainly true. But we cannot ignore the human instinct for self-preservation which lay under those excuses. However, I shall not argue the merit or demerit of it, or what they did. We simply think of those who went to the battlefield as having fought off the same desire for self-preservation that they also had somewhere in their hearts and minds as those who avoided the military duty. The ideas of fighting "for the nation" and "for the Emperor" were a heavy

157

burden pressing on their hearts and minds. Since they loved their fatherland and their home, most of them gladly accepted their fate and went to the battlefield. Some even flew single planes and then courageously dove into an enemy battleship, believing in the immortality of the "Emperor."

Perhaps even a more poignant case would be someone who survived by stubbornly refusing to volunteer to be a member of the Special Attack Forces while in the Air Corps. Scorned as a traitor and an enemy conspirator by superior officers, and ridiculed by colleagues as a coward, he absolutely refused to volunteer (to be a member of the Special Attack Force). . . .

In this way some survived the war.

Now that the powder smoke is gone, we survivors can think back on those dark days. During that period, we also shared exactly the same emotions that fill this book. I am not saying, however, that all of us were thinking of the war and death in the same way during the war. Some grasped the true nature of the war, and were challenging it, but a great many people believed in the war as the beautiful slogan that was given to them, and burnt their young bodies and souls to win a victory. In a way, this was inevitable for those of us who had been brought up under an unprecedented suppression of ideologies ever since our childhood. Now that the true nature of the war as imperialistic aggression has become so clear under the sun, our thinking in those days seems so very childlike and naïve, and the expressions we used may also have been tongue-tied (i.e., far from eloquent). Some may dismiss that as things of the pre-modern era, but I want you (the reader) to at least be clearly aware of the following points. To begin with, we were always thinking seriously, and we never lost our humanity during the war regardless of how horrible the war got. We were even looking with the eyes of deep love at the enemy nations, although we had to kill each other just because we were born as different nationalities (i.e., the members of different nations). Even though it was not clearly understood, what we were really hating was something that was hovering over us like a dark cloud—something that forced us to kill those we did not hate.

Some among us were tired of reading the type of books which were permitted under the hideously oppressive Thought-Control Police. We could not continue serious thinking any more, and so we entered the military in the vague hope that actions (or, being actively involved in something) might yield results. But the military was not that sort of an easy place. It was filled with all sorts of dishonor and corruption. None of our freedom was recognized there. They certainly did not even pay any attention to our humanity (i.e., our humanity was never even considered). However, for those young people who were filled with the principles of justice and conscience, it was only natural that *ningen-sei* (humanity/humanism) should first be born and then maintained in their hearts. So the sacred fire of humanity/humanism, which always lives deep inside human beings at any time and under any circumstances, did not die in our hearts. You, the reader, will find numerous examples of that in this book. Also, I believe, you will shed your tears for the students killed in the war for their humanity/humanism which turned out to be so fleeting and fragile for them (if we look at it from the end result). I would think that we ought to return to that point once again and make it the spiritual foundation for Japan's reconstruction.

When the war ended what we felt so strongly, more than anything else, was the simple fact that we had survived. That powerful emotion immediately spread over the defeated fatherland. That reconstruction of the fatherland, or rather, more accurately, the creation of a new Japan, was the most important duty for all of us who survived the war —we felt that with our whole hearts and souls. Actually, many of us were quietly and secretly anticipating this day even before the end of the war.

It was for that reason that the survivors dared not join the Special Attack Forces. It was not just because they did not want to die, or that they casually sat back and saw friends fly off. They were not coldly watching with disdain those of full youthful vigor, but were confident that their own action was the correct one. They too were human though, and so were not watching with hearts of stone those who flew off, carrying bombs in their chests. They cried. They were in pain and agony. Yet, they did not volunteer (to join the Special Attack Forces); their true hearts did not allow them to do so.

This was the way in which we survived the war, but this collection of writings also contains several pieces which were written by members of the Special Attack Forces just before they left for their sorties. When we read these and imagine the faces of those numerous young people who were killed in the war, we cannot help but think that we all share something that permeates our minds—our fate was simply much too dark. Under that black cloud each of us had to think alone and to be distressed alone. We were not allowed to discuss matters with one

another. Therefore, all alone, each of us had to make a move either forward or backward. Oh, how well I remember the eyes of those (who
were flying off) who silently looked at those of us who came to say
goodbye. Were we the only ones who recognized the lonely and faintly troubled *hikari* (light, glow) of humanity that they never lost, and
which was revealed in the depths of their clear and lonely-looking
eyes? Is this a subjective view whereby only we as compilers read
between the lines of their writings to find something so beautiful and
precious, and in which all of us have a share?

If we think this way, we can begin to understand what those who
went away to fight the war and died expected of us who are left behind.
At the moment we realized that we had survived the war, we understood that (i.e., what they expected of us). Most certainly, not all of us
who survived the war had any clear intention of doing so. Some regret-
ted the country's defeat and said that they should have died, and some
may have survived just because of blind fate. But there were also those
(perhaps there are more of them than the others) who must have awakened soon after their realization of having survived the war. I am sure
that they too came up with the great burning desire to do something,
but we humans tend to choose the easier path. We were likely to soon
forget such strong emotions as well as our original determination, and
tended to be absorbed in the licentious quality to the whole post-war
atmosphere. I believe that the prime function of this collection of writings is to bring back once again, and in the most genuine way, the feeling that "we survived the war." We tend to forget this fact too easily.

There is a book similar to this one, entitled *Doitsu Senbotsu
Gakusei no Tegami* (*Letters of the Fallen German Students*). (This is a
Japanese translation of selected pieces from *Kriegsbriefe gefullener
Studenten*, compiled after World War I by Professor Philipp Witcop of
Freiburg University.) Many of the writers in our collection made men-
tion of this book: and they all stated that they read the book with certain strong emotions. That book certainly is worthy of such emotions,
but we would like to recommend (to our readers) our collection even
more than that book. Especially with regard to our methods of compilation, we are confident that our work is many degrees superior to
Professor Witcop's. While he aimed at instilling in the reader the idea
of German supremacy, our primary goal was to bring forward humanity itself. It is true that the writings we gathered into this book contain
no piece describing harsh battlefield scenes. This may be due to the
extremely strict Japanese military censorship (under which these

pieces were written). In this regard, we suppose that *Doitsu Senbotsu Gakusei no Tegami* is far more vivid than this collection. What we wish to point out, however, is the poverty of ideologies (among those student-authors) in Germany—a poverty of thought among the youth in spite of the (historical) fact that Germany produced so many great philosophers and thinkers. We wonder whether or not this may have been the reason the German people allowed Nazism to rise within twenty years (after WWI). We are not insisting that the writings contained in *this* book are so rich in profound ideologies. What we want to say is simply that, even though we (the authors and Japanese university students in general) were not free to express our thoughts, we held on to the freedom to think as powerfully as this collection indicates. That is, our classmates had at least this freedom to think. We who, to a greater or lesser extent, shared the same environment as they did, can find in their writings enough keen and poignant thought to make tears well up. It does not matter how badly we may have been suppressed, so long as we had this liberty (i.e., the freedom to think), since sooner or later *shinri* (the truth) will inevitably sprout out.

Unfortunately, they (the authors of this book) could not live to see this *shinri* bear fruit, but we, by standing on (the foundation of) the same "freedom to think," begin a brand new start now. When and where this freedom exists, truth shall always fly out like the phoenix from the ash. We find this foundation for reconstruction already present in these wartime writings. We believe a country which is responsible for producing these people (i.e., the authors) is in no danger of destruction.

Although the dark atmosphere that our fallen students had to suffer is now completely wiped out, we are now the victims of a new type of suffering which they knew nothing about. By this I mean the reality which the country must confront after our defeat. We face inflation, unemployment, the black market, and all sorts of values being turned upside-down. The social unrest which results—and also the pessimism and decadence which are inevitable by-products of this post-war situation—are now rampant. The social condition for us today is truly filled with all sorts of pains and difficulties. However, we must overcome them. We survived the war—we survived in order to overcome (our society's difficulties). To create a new Japan would be the only and the best memorial for those students killed in the war. In that sense, can these writings that we have compiled be a source for overcoming the crisis (we are now facing)? Be the matter what it may. . . .

We survived the war; throughout that harsh war somehow we survived, and we should never forget the true meaning of the fact that we did so.

> This Postscript was first drafted by Kikuo Nomoto, a member of the editorial committee of the Senbotsu Gakusei Shuki Henshūki Iinkai (Committee for the Compilation of Writings of the Students Killed in the War) of the Tō-dai Gakusei Jichikai (The University of Tokyo Student Autonomous Society, or Student Council), and then completed in consultation with other committee members.

AUTHORS INDEX